W9-AAL-607

CRIME SCENE INVESTIGATION

Thomas F. Adams
Professor Emeritus, Criminal Justice
Santa Ana College, Santa Ana, California
Former Lieutenant, Santa Ana Police Department

Jeffrey L. Krutsinger
Forensic Specialist II
Santa Ana Police Department

Library of Congress Cataloging-in-Publication Data

Adams, Thomas Francis
 Crime scene investigation / Thomas F. Adams, Jeffrey Lee
Krutsinger.
  p. cm.
 Includes bibliographical references.
 ISBN 0-13-593427-3
 1. Crime scene searches. 2. Criminal investigation. 3. Evidence,
Criminal. I. Krutsinger, Jeffrey Lee. II. Title.
 HV8073.A528 2000
 363.25'2--dc21
                  99-27459
                   CIP

Acquisitions Editor: *Neil Marquardt*
Director of Production and Manufacturing: *Bruce Johnson*
Production Editor/Formatting/Interior Design: *Denise Brown*
Manufacturing Buyer: *Ed O'Dougherty*
Managing Editor: *Mary Carnis*
Editorial Assistant: *Susan M. Kegler*
Creative Director: *Marianne Frasco*
Senior Design Coordinator: *Miguel Ortiz*
Cover Design: *Thomas F. Adams*
Marketing Manager: *Shannon Simonsen*
Printer/Binder: *RR Donnelley & Sons/Harrisonburg*

©2000 by Prentice-Hall, Inc.
Upper Saddle River, New Jersey 07458

All rights reserved. No part of this book may be
reproduced, in any form or by any means,
without permission in writing from the publisher.

Unless otherwise noted all photos are courtesy of the Santa Ana Police Department.

Printed in the United States of America

10 9 8 7 6 5 4 3 2 1

ISBN 0-13-593427-3

Prentice-Hall International (UK) Limited, *London*
Prentice-Hall of Australia Pty. Limited, *Sydney*
Prentice-Hall Canada Inc., *Toronto*
Prentice-Hall Hispanoamericana, S.A., *Mexico*
Prentice-Hall of India Private Limited, *New Delhi*
Prentice-Hall of Japan, Inc., *Tokyo*
Pearson Education Asia Pte. Ltd., *Singapore*
Editora Prentice-Hall do Brasil, Ltda., *Rio de Janeiro*

Brian, this one is for you,
with love from your proud dad.

TFA

Contents

Preface

The headlines blare: "DEFENSE ATTORNEY CHALLENGES THE POLICE EVIDENCE IN MURDER TRIAL, charge the police with planting and sloppy handling of the evidence." Stop! Back up! How did that happen? We did everything exactly according to the book. Unfortunately, that's the problem. We must rewrite the book.

For many years, as crime scene investigators, we collected the evidence, took the photos, prepared the reports, and eventually presented the evidence in court. Hardly ever did anyone, especially defense lawyers, challenge our motives or our methods. We did our job as professionals do. It was a debatable presumption, we believe, that a job done professionally was presumed to have been done correctly.

Then something happened. Attorneys found that by challenging the evidence and the way it was collected and handled, and suggesting that perhaps the evidence collector had some ulterior motive, the case could be won by raising sufficient reasonable doubt about how the entire case was handled. This was not a new tactic, but with the mega-publicity blitz given the so-called "trial of the century" and the alleged "dream team" of defense attorneys, other attorneys have taken the baton and are running with it.

The purpose of this book is to focus on the basics of crime scene investigation. Not only must the crime scene investigators perform a perfect job, but their work must appear to have been done perfectly by strictly unbiased investigators searching for the proof. The crime scene investigator is not an advocate, and should make every effort not to appear as one.

When I, co-author Adams, first started working on this project it soon became apparent that it would be worthless without taking on board a currently working crime scene specialist who would collaborate on the final phases of the writing, but his principal contribution would be as a photographer. With the collaboration of co-author Krutsinger, I believe we have come up with what is the best text on crime scene investigation on the market today. Actually, we found that this subject is usually relegated to just one or two chapters of a more comprehensive text of Criminal Investigation procedures, and we could find no current publication devoted exclusively to this one subject. We believe this book fills that void.

ACKNOWLEDGMENTS

Special thanks to Santa Ana, CA Police Chief Paul M. Walters, who authorized Jeff Krutsinger's participation in this project as co-author (who produced most of the photographs in this book). Two former editors of Prentice Hall, Jack Pritchard and Bob Howland, are responsible for the first few texts by author Adams, and two relative newcomers to PH, Kim Davies and Neil Marquardt were the facilitators for this book with the addition of co-author Krutsinger. Thanks for your faith and encouragement.

Special thanks to our mentors, instructors, and colleagues who inspired us and through example and other media have been instrumental in our development in the fine art and science of crime scene investigation. Thanks also to our colleagues who do their jobs in a professional manner and make us look as though we know what we are writing about.

Chapter One
Overview

INTRODUCTION

You have been assigned to investigate the scene of a crime that just recently occurred in your jurisdiction. You may or may not have done this before, and investigation of such scenes may or may not be a regular part of your duty assignment. Whatever the case, the success or failure of the investigation is largely up to you, because the initial phases of any criminal investigation most often determine the final outcome. How you conduct the investigation will directly affect all that follows, up to and including the eventual prosecution of the perpetrator(s). Once you have completed your work at the scene, the tapes and barricades removed, and the premises returned to the occupants, you will never be able to go back and do the job again. Oh, you may return to pick up the pieces, but the scene will change and will never be identical to the condition in which you found it when you first arrived and secured the scene.

In this text we intend to provide the information you need to guide you through the initial crime scene investigation from beginning to end, with the objective of assuring you and your colleagues that your investigation is as thorough and complete as possible, which will lead to a successful follow-up investigation and conclusion. Another case cleared.

PRESUMPTION OF EFFICIENCY

According to the rules of evidence, it is a rebuttable presumption that the work you do as a professional peace officer in the course of your official duties is done correctly and thoroughly. If you have read enough fiction, you probably have gathered that all police officers perform their duties according to the book and never make mistakes (well, hardly ever).

Unfortunately, that is one of the great myths about police work. *Many times, far more than we want to believe, officers do make mistakes, and sometimes very serious ones at that.* What you must do is to develop a correct routine, which varies from case to case, but a routine nevertheless that will assure everyone involved in the case that you have performed your job correctly and completely. It may be necessary to develop your own checklist to use during your investigation to assure complete investigations. Before they leave the ground, experienced and well-trained pilots and crewmembers religiously use checklists to assure a safe flight for themselves and their passengers. So should you prepare and use checklists to assure thorough investigations before you leave the premises of a crime scene.

ANTICIPATE CRITICAL REVIEW OF YOUR WORK

You should be the toughest critic of your own investigative work. After the dust has cleared and you have completed your phase of the investigation, review and evaluate what you have done. Make notes on what you should have done that you did not do, or should have done better, and how your next crime scene investigation will be more thorough. There will be critics galore both within and outside your department. Your supervisors, the follow-up investigators, division chiefs, and even the chief executive of your department will be reviewing and evaluating your work. Then there are the prosecutors who you will sometimes feel are actually on the "other side" because they find fault with your work, as they often play "devil's advocate" in anticipation of the defense attorneys' tactics, who will attack your work every step of the way in order to get evidence excluded or the case dismissed on behalf of their clients. Of course, the defense attorneys will find fault with your work even when there is none to find, because they can, and because that's the very serious game they play to assure adequate representation of their clients.

Then there are the appeals that follow conviction, providing one was obtained. Trial judges, appeals court justices, and even the honorable justices of the state Supreme Court and/or the U.S. Supreme Court may have a crack at reviewing the work that you and your colleagues did investigating the crime scene. Sometimes a convicted defendant will have his or her conviction overturned because of what you might choose to call a "technicality," which actually may be what some or all of those individuals see as inadequate or improper performance by you and your colleagues.

THE FOURTH AMENDMENT

The Fourth Amendment of the Bill of Rights, which protects persons and places from unreasonable searches and seizures by agents of the government, does not apply to the basic crime scene, which by circumstance has opened itself up to careful scrutiny by you and others directly involved in the criminal investigation. It falls within the "reasonable cause" category when you are at the scene of a crime, and the goal of your search is to determine the nature of the crime, to find all of the evidence necessary to prove all of the elements of the crime, and to identify the person or persons responsible for the crime. It is also reasonable to identify the victim and all of the circumstances about the person and/or place that is the object of the attack. In other words, it is only a very rare circumstance when you will need a warrant to conduct a crime scene search.

If and when the occasion arises for you to seek a search warrant from the local magistrate, the affidavit must state where you wish to search, including the exact address, an accurate description of the place, exactly what you expect to find, and what reliable information you have that leads you to believe that the search will yield the evidence that you expect to find. Once you have the warrant in hand, then you may proceed with the search, which should be consistent with what you expect to find. For example, if you are searching the residence of a burglary suspect for small tools used to gain entry and several handguns, it would not be logical to search places where one would not be likely to find those objects, such as in the pages of a paperback book or a diary. But let us get back to the crime scene. Search warrant procedures are covered in other texts in much greater detail. If in doubt about any aspect of any search that you conduct, seek the counsel and advice of your department's legal counsel or the prosecuting attorney.

EVIDENTIARY VALUES

All of the evidence that you will collect and eventually present in court falls into two basic categories: direct and circumstantial. Although some people will argue that one has more value than the other does, actually they are both of variable value, depending on their own unique set of circumstances about how and when the items of evidence are collected. On its face, direct evidence, such as an eyewitness account of robbery and identification of the robber in a lineup by the eyewitness, would appear to be about the best evidence you can get in a robbery case. But, what if your eyewitness was intoxicated at the time of the crime and has a history of allegedly being present during various crimes and exaggerating his own involvement in such cases when talking to the police? Eyewitnesses are known to make mistakes; therefore, this bit of direct evidence is of questionable value at best. Compare that with a set of fingerprints left on the cash register by the robber at the time of the crime, which positively identifies the culprit as the owner of the prints. That item of circumstantial evidence appears to have much more value than the first example. You must evaluate not only the evidence but also the source and the means by which it came into your possession.

Actually, most facts in a criminal case are proven by circumstantial evidence, and it is not possible to state that direct evidence is in all cases better or worse than circumstantial evidence. All evidence is important, and each item or bit of information that lies in the category of evidence must be regarded as though it were the most crucial element of the investigation. Sometimes it is not until months later that what seemed to be an inconsequential item would prove to be the single most important element of the case. In some cases, judges or jurors may determine in their own minds what convinced them of the defendant's guilt or innocence. Consider, if you will, the 1995 trial of Orenthal J. Simpson, when the jury completely disregarded some of the most overwhelming evidence, which would have convicted anyone else of double homicide, and found him "not guilty" in spite of the evidence.

Because nothing is absolute in the field of evidence, the experts always speak of reliability of evidence in terms of probabilities. A fingerprint expert will never state that the latent prints found at the crime scene are positively those of the suspect as a result of comparing the latents with a rolled set of comparison prints taken in the office or found in the files of the FBI or another agency. What the expert will say is that the probability that the latents were left by someone other than the defendant is about one in 100 million. In other words, of the 100 million sets of fingerprints searched, only one set of prints, those of the defendant, matched the latents found at the crime scene. So far, in all the years that fingerprint files have been maintained worldwide, no two people have come up with identical sets of prints.

Take DNA, or deoxyribonucleic acid, for example. Of the current world population of about 5 billion people, some experts have proclaimed that no two people—except for identical twins—have the same DNA, or genetic code. The mathematical probability of duplicate genetic codes, with the exception of identical (not fraternal) twins, would be 5 billion to one. Of course, the scientists have not cataloged the DNA of all 5 billion inhabitants on earth but use projected mathematical probabilities not unlike opinion polls. An oversimplified example of such a poll would be that 100 Republicans randomly selected and 100 similarly selected

Democrats (in this case allegedly representing all the Republicans and Democrats in a given area) are asked if they favor "three strikes and you're out" laws. Eighty-five Republicans and 85 Democrats state that they are in favor of the law. The pollsters would then project that 85 percent of all Democrats and Republicans believe the law is a good one. If they question 10 more of each and come up with a different breakdown, the results will change. For instance, if someone is fingerprinted or yields a DNA sample and is found to be identical to another person, then the odds for fingerprints would be one in 50 million or DNA would be one in 2.5 billion. Scientifically speaking, those are still pretty good odds.

CRITERIA FOR DETERMINING EVIDENTIARY VALUES

1. *Mathematical probability.* As long as every attempt to replicate an examination to produce identical results comes up negative, the criminalist can say that of 3,000 attempts to produce an identical result, it did not happen a single time. Therefore, the probability of matching two pieces of broken glass as in a jigsaw puzzle, and being able to duplicate a match of one of those pieces of broken glass with another is 1 : 3,000 because of the 3,000 unsuccessful attempts by the criminalist. So it can be said with some scientific certainty (but not absolutely) that two pieces of broken glass that fit together in all likelihood came from the same pane of glass and that they were previously both part of one piece, and now there are two that fit together at the place they were separated.

    Here are a couple of other examples. When you toss a coin, the probability that it will come up "heads" is one in two, 1 : 2 (because there are two sides to the coin). If 40 percent of all humans have type O blood, you can say that two of every five people have type O blood. Even if you come up with five people in a row who have type O blood, the probability will not change because so many people have had their blood typed, and of all of those individuals, 40 percent of humans have type O blood. If you have type A blood, what is the probability that the next time your blood is typed it will be anything other than A? Zero, of course, because blood type does not change.

2. *Uniqueness.* A shoe print that appears to have been made by a size twelve shoe is found impressed in the soil in a flower bed

outside the murder victim's bedroom window. The design of the print on the sole, including a logo and some type of lettering, is characteristic of only one type of shoe custom made by a shoemaker in Milan, Italy, according to the shoe print expert of the Federal Bureau of Investigation. No other shoemaker can be found who manufactures a shoe with a similar design. The victim's son wears a size twelve shoe, and you find in a search of his apartment a sales slip showing that the son bought a pair of size twelve shoes from that same shoemaker in Milan. How many people wear size twelve shoes? How many people known to the victim wear size twelve shoes? How many people purchased size twelve shoes from that particular shoemaker in Milan? Further examination of the shoe print shows a distinctive wear pattern and a cut across the heel impression that appears to have been made by a knife. You find the son's size twelve shoes and one of the shoes appears to have similar wear pattern, logo, and lettering design, and one of the shoes has a knife cut across the heel. The shoe expert will point out the similarities between the shoe and the impression that it probably made, and the improbability of any two shoes making an identical impression, but he or she will never say that a specific shoe made that specific impression. Yet the situation is so unique that it can hardly be attributed to coincidence.

3. *Inconsistency.* A middle-age rape victim who has lived alone for the past twenty years, who does not smoke and has never allowed anyone to smoke in her house, finds a half-smoked cigar in her bathroom sink. It is reasonable to assume that the intruder was the one who brought the cigar to the scene and left it behind because of its inconsistency with the victim's lifestyle. In an embezzlement case, the office manager started working late every night without asking for overtime pay and at the same time volunteered to take care of the bank deposits. One of the clerks at the bank became suspicious when the office manager opened a second account with himself as the signator, which was inconsistent with the company's previous banking practices. After the office manager started making withdrawals from the second account, the bank employees became suspicious and phoned the owner of the company, who subsequently went to the police department and filed

a complaint against the office manager for embezzlement of several thousand dollars. The manager had coincidentally taken an unscheduled vacation (which was also inconsistent with his behavior of never wanting to take time off for vacations or even illness).

4. *Physical match.* The perpetrator of a "smash and grab" burglary broke a window. Fragments of glass taken out of a suspect's clothing were compared with the glass still remaining in the window, both as to physical characteristics and mechanical match, and the criminalist's expert opinion was that the glass fragments found on the suspect were probably—with little chance for doubt—part of the broken plate of glass. The mechanical match was made by photographing the larger fragments that have a shape to them and photographing the remnants of the window at the scene, and moving the photographs around as one would put together a jigsaw puzzle, coming up with a match. It is virtually impossible for any two sheets of glass to be broken in exactly the same way. Virtually, but not absolutely. We are dealing with the law of probabilities again.

CORPUS DELICTI, THE ELEMENTS OF THE CRIME

When you respond to the crime scene, not only keep in mind what type of crime has been reported but also keep your mind open to the possibility that the evidence may show you that the crime is not as originally reported, or that one crime, such as arson, was committed to cover up another crime, such as murder. It is possible that another type of crime altogether was committed, or your investigation may prove that there was no crime at all. That's why the investigation must be as thorough as possible. Let the evidence present itself to you and then determine what crime, if any, occurred. A very common error in communication is when a burglary victim comes home and reports to the police that he or she has been "robbed." Even the media writers and reporters often confuse the two completely different types of crimes.

As you know, each of the disparate elements of the corpus delicti must be proven by reliable and constitutionally admissible evidence. You cannot infer that evidence exists; you must prove that such evidence exists by legally presenting it in court. Often defense attorneys will challenge testimony and evidence that they are able to review prior to the trial by means of discovery.

DISCOVERY

All information and evidence that you discover during the investigation must be revealed to the defense, and the defense must also reveal to the prosecution what evidence and information it has, with the exception of those items that may be withheld to assure the defendant's Fifth Amendment rights not to be a witness against oneself. Although not a game, the discovery process is similar to playing a hand of poker where all players must show the others their cards. Under such conditions it would be rather hard to bluff the others with the impression that one player is holding a royal flush when they can see only a pair of eights. When the defense attorneys see that your evidence is weak—which they believe does not prove an element of the corpus delicti or which they believe was collected in violation of the search and seizure rules, or *Miranda* in the case of statements or admissions obtained—they are going to petition the court for a pretrial hearing to suppress that evidence so that it cannot be presented later at the trial.

So what you have here are several tests along the way before an item of evidence may be allowed to serve its purpose to prove an element of the crime. The bottom line is that every item of evidence must be carefully collected, meticulously packaged and transported to the evidence repository, or the laboratory, carefully analyzed by the laboratory technicians and criminalists, transported to the courtroom for the trial, and legally presented in court. All of this has to be within the strict confines of the rules for maintaining a continuous and unbroken chain of custody.

LIABILITY PROTECTION

We operate in a world filled with litigation-happy people and a legion of hungry attorneys. Be careful to protect yourself and your department from lawsuits when the property owners and even the victims whose crimes you are investigating claim that you or your colleagues destroyed or stole their valuable property while investigating the crime scene or searching other places for evidence. Even though you are the "nice guys"—helping out the victims by working to solve their crimes, recovering their property, and prosecuting the "bad guys"—it brings out the greed in people when they see a chance to cash in on some "big bucks," and their attorneys can pay the rent for a few more months. Some victims will blame the investigators when the case goes awry, and it is not unusual to encounter suspects who will file a lawsuit in hopes of using it as a bargaining chip to negotiate for the police and prosecution to drop or reduce the criminal charges against them.

You and your department represent "deep pockets," into which these litigants and their attorneys seek to reach and fill their own pockets, sometimes garnering the sympathy of jurors who tend to sympathize with "underdogs" who are victimized by bureaucrats. You must anticipate that such lawsuits are going to be filed against you no matter how meticulous and honest you are. For that reason, be careful to document everything that you do, see, and say throughout the investigation.

Depending on your department's human and financial resources, consider adding to the team of crime scene investigators a videographer–historian whose sole purpose is to memorialize the entire investigation from beginning to end. If the date and time feature on the camcorder is available, be sure of the accuracy of the date and time the tape is being made. In one so-called "crime of the century," the O.J. Simpson case, a videographer recorded scenes of the suspect's house for liability protection purposes yet caused some serious credibility problems when the date and time showing on the tape were different than when he and other officers testified he made the tapes. That seemingly inconsequential matter, which the videographer overlooked when checking out the camcorder, gave the defense team some good ammunition with which to attack the prosecution's case.

THEORY OF TRANSFER

Although many cases may cause you to question your faith in the theory of transfer, always consider the possibility that perpetrators often take something away from a crime scene and leave something there, although it may be only a memory. You don't have to be a psychic to feel someone's presence at a crime scene without knowing what you are sensing, and then to have a dé jà vu experience when you are later face-to-face in the same person's actual presence. Sometimes the odor of a person's cologne or aftershave lotion lingers at the scene, or the pungent and distinct aroma of a particular type of pipe or cigar tobacco permeates the crime scene, especially if it is an enclosed space. Then later, when you are in that person's presence, you may smell the same odor and not even be aware of what is happening. That's a more subtle type of transference, which is not likely to serve as presentable evidence in court, but it may help narrow down your list of suspects.

Look for items that the culprit may have left behind at the crime scene. Fingerprints, shoe impressions, and traces of body fluids are what you are most likely to search for. Also consider discarded cigarette butts outside the point of entry, or candy or chewing gum wrappers, tools or weapons, or broken bits of tools damaged while prying at safe doors, metal drawers, or doors. The culprit may not only take the "loot" from a crime scene but also may take food or beverages from the refrigerator, tools or weapons found at the scene, or other items he or she might consider souvenirs. Part of your investigative routine should be to expect proof of your transference theory.

CHAIN OF CONTINUITY OR CUSTODY

It will be your responsibility to guarantee the integrity of the unbroken chain of custody from the very moment an item of evidence is found until it reaches its final destination at the evidence locker or the laboratory; and then again when the item goes from one of those places to the courtroom. While the evidence is in the custody of the evidence custodians or the laboratory technicians, those individuals will share the responsibility for its continuity. Then, when it comes time for court presentation, it will be up to you to take the evidence to the court and present it at the trial with a complete explanation of its itinerary. No evidence can be introduced without a human's testimony to make it a part of the trial. Any persons who have no official business with an item of evidence should *never* handle it, or else the chain is broken. Once the chain has been broken, the integrity of the evidence is in jeopardy.

In order to assure an unbroken chain, each item of evidence should be tagged with what amounts to a tracking slip, such as that used by Federal Express or United Parcel Service to keep track of a package while enroute as well as to document its arrival. The original holder of the evidence should affix the tag with the correct information, which we will cover in a later chapter. Then, every person whose hands the item passes through will add his or her "link" to the chain with name as well as date and time received and passed on. If a link in the chain is missing, you will have to testify to that during the trial. Suppose you found a revolver of a specific description at the crime scene, yet because you cannot account for the gun's journey from link K to link N, you must say that the weapon appears to be the same one. But you cannot be certain, you see, because somewhere you have lost links L and M.

MEDIA RELATIONS

The public has a right to know that you are doing your job by investigating crimes for the purpose of locating the perpetrators and bringing them to justice. The public does not have a right to know the details of a case under investigation that would jeopardize the successful conclusion of your investigation, no matter what the media representatives will try to argue. "Scoops," "exclusives," and ratings are not your responsibility. Do not fall into the trap of feeling that you must pander to the media to get their cooperation. It is your duty to be polite and respectful, and to refer the media to your supervisors or to the department's media liaison person. Certain unscrupulous news reporters will create their own story completely or will give it their own slant, depending on that agency's editorial policies. Just because they print or broadcast misinformation, perhaps to bait you into giving them the "correct information," don't fall into their trap. Your job is to investigate the crime scene, not to act as a news reporter.

In a very high-profile case, such as a spectacular murder or a crime involving celebrities, be careful to shield the crime scene from the cameras in the helicopters above or in the trees or on top of buildings down the street. There are some media people who set out to conduct their own investigation and to question suspects and witnesses so that they may *make* their own news rather than report it. How many times have you seen good cases compromised or literally destroyed because of premature release of information, or misinformation?

Sometimes it is necessary for your media relations people to ask the print and broadcast people to withhold certain information that they may have in the interest of common decency so that the follow-up investigators may go after the perpetrator(s) and interrogate them for their knowledge of the crime. Consider the case where only the victim (who is dead), the coroner's people, the investigators, and the murderer know what weapon was used and where it was disposed of after the crime. Later, when the suspect confesses to the crime and describes the weapon and what he did with it, you will know with some reliability that you have the right suspect. But, consider how the case would be compromised if all that information were publicized and you would not know for sure if you had the true confessor or a false confessor. Yes, there are many people who confess to crimes they never committed for a variety of reasons. Just ask the "old-timers" on your department.

SUMMARY

In this overview chapter, we have covered many topics, some of which we will discuss in more detail later in the book. It is absolutely essential that your investigation be thorough and complete. Although some people generally presume that a well-trained police officer does good work as a matter of routine, we know that all officers are not equally efficient and that many make serious errors in spite of their training. For that reason, you should expect critical review of your work from many directions. Although the Fourth Amendment rules concerning search and seizure do not generally apply to crime scene investigations, there are many ancillary searches when you may have to adhere to the rules closely.

All elements of the crime, or the *corpus delicti*, must be proven in order for you to establish that a crime has, in fact, been committed and these elements are proven by either direct or by circumstantial evidence. Evidentiary values of certain objects or information vary with each situation, but in this chapter we have discussed some of the criteria for determining those values. Keep in mind that the rules of discovery require that both prosecution and defense share information so that there are few secrets prior to and during the trial.

We rounded out the chapter with discussions of the theory of transfer and the chain of evidence custody precautions to take to avoid accusations of theft or damage to the property of victims or other persons involved in your investigations, and one of the most important topics of all: media relations. We are public servants and need to keep the public informed about our activities, but certain information must be withheld to assure the confidentiality of our cases until the facts are presented at the appropriate time in court. Sometimes this puts us at odds with certain members of the media, who are pushed to the limits by their editors and station managers to beat the competition with "exclusives" and "first on the scene" situations. Leave this to the media experts in your own department and keep your own counsel, limiting your reporting to your reports and to your supervisors.

SUGGESTED OUTSIDE PROJECTS

1. Meet with the media relations expert in your local police or sheriff's department and obtain, if possible, a copy of the media relations guidelines. Using that document as your base, develop what you believe to be a workable policy statement on media relations for that agency.

2. Prepare a list of examples of criteria for determining evidentiary values in each of the categories of mathematical probability, uniqueness, inconsistency, and evidentiary match.

DISCUSSION QUESTIONS

1. How do you see the difference between direct and circumstantial evidence? Can you come up with a convincing argument that one is better than the others are?

2. What do you know about DNA and the state of the art at the present time?

3. Can you give an example of any type of evidence that may be regarded as positive proof of a fact?

4. What do the agencies in your geographical area do to protect themselves against malpractice of their officers in crime scene investigations?

5. Describe the chain of custody process in an average crime scene investigation.

6. Describe the theory of transfer, and give an example of how this might work in a convenience store robbery case.

7. Explain the process known as "discovery." Which side benefits most from the discovery rules, prosecution or defense?

8. What do you think about the crime scene investigator using a checklist to assure a thorough investigation?

9. If the Fourth Amendment protects people from intrusive practices of government officials, what protection is there against intrusive private persons who force entries and conduct searches on their own?

10. Describe the process for getting a search warrant.

Chapter Two
The Crime Scene Kit

INTRODUCTION

Your crime scene investigation (CSI) kit should contain all of the equipment and supplies listed and discussed in this chapter, plus any additional items we may have missed or items that you consider necessary to suit your individual style. In the larger department, you may be fortunate to have enough money in the budget to have a fully equipped crime scene van or truck.

In that case, your equipment and supply list will include the kit, plus additional pieces of equipment, such as ladders, lighting, generators and refrigerator to preserve perishable items, and other conveniences. The regular crime scene kit should be compact and capable of being carried in the trunk of a police cruiser.

Figure 2.1 Minivans are excellent for use as a crime scene investigation vehicle because they have plenty of room for tools and evidence.

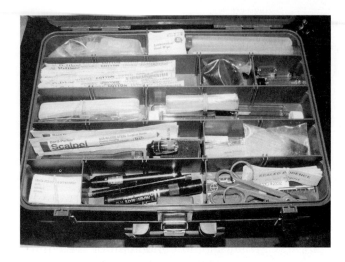

Figure 2.2 Fishing tackle boxes are excellent for making a field CSI kit.

THE IDEAL CRIME SCENE KIT

When stocking your kit, use this chapter as a basis for developing your checklist of essential items. The list does not list items in order of importance.

1. Traffic flares and cyalume wands for traffic diversion at street or highway scenes. These items can be used to close off a traffic lane or sidewalk or as nighttime hand signals. Barricades and cones should be in the storeroom at headquarters or in the CSI van.

2. Yellow plastic tape with or without "POLICE LINE DO NOT CROSS" lettering for designating the boundaries and restricting access to the scene. If you have large populations of people whose first language is not English, use tapes printed in one or more of those languages.

3. Lights. A variety of lighting devices such as penlights, flashlights, floodlights, battery-powered lanterns with red and amber lenses to serve as warning or stoplights.

4. Small portable generator for alternating current and an ample supply of batteries of various sizes for the direct current–powered lights, and converters to accommodate variations in power sources.

5. Ultraviolet and infrared lights for examining trace evidence at the scene, such as latent prints on multicolored surfaces, fluids

Figure 2.3   UV lights are used to look for many types of trace evidence.

that fluoresce under ultraviolet, and other substances that reveal themselves under infrared lights.

6. Report forms, spiral bound notebook, and ballpoint pen with black ink.

7. Clipboard with graph paper and pencils, and templates used for drawing items such as vehicles, furniture, and other items commonly depicted in crime and accident scene sketches.

8. Chalk, marking pens, and other marking devices, including markers for wet surfaces, and spray paint.

Figure 2.4   A possy box like this one serves not only as a clipboard but also as a place to store film, forms, and other tools.

Figure 2.5   Large number placards are helpful to mark and identify evidence at a crime scene.

9.   Numbered and lettered tags and placards and tented cards to locate certain items of evidence.

10.   Steel measuring tape and wood or plastic ruler. Avoid the use of cloth measuring tapes, which stretch or shrink.

11.   Evidence cards and labels with accurate ruler printed along the edge.

12.   Compass for determining true north, which should appear in all sketches and photographs when possible. A North arrow imprinted on a 3 × 5 card and placed in the scene where possible will aid the viewer in establishing directions in the scene.

Figure 2.6   Rulers and scales of all sizes are vital to show size and position of evidence. Some scales are magnetic or come as stickers. The L-shape ruler is vital when photographing shoe prints. All long tape measures should be metal in order to assure that no stretching occurs.

Figure 2.7 A good 35mm single lens reflex camera with a zoom lens and powerful flash is probably one of the crime scene investigator's best tools.

13. Polaroid and/or digital camera for immediate feedback on your photographs, and to serve as a backup in case some of the more sophisticated camera equipment does not work.

14. 35mm single lens reflex (SLR) camera for most, if not all, of your still photos of the scene, as well as tripods, various lenses, and accessories for a variety of photo situations.

15. High-quality and high-speed film.

16. Fingerprint camera for one-to-one close-ups of fingerprints and other trace evidence.

17. Video camcorder. If you are working alone, the voice recorder feature will enhance your ability to record the crime scene both visually and orally as you keep a running dialogue while you go through the scene. If you do not wish to use the sound feature, turn it off before you start recording to avoid having embarrassing comments and other sounds come out later on, which might be made by those not aware that the sound is rolling. Date and time feature should be correct if you use it.

18. Gloves. Heavy rubber gloves for working around electricity, heavy work gloves for lifting and other heavy work, and thin latex gloves for most of your work handling evidence. Carry

several pairs of the latex gloves, as they should be changed frequently to avoid cross-contaminating items you handle, such as blood-covered items.

19. Plastic shoe covers, or "booties." These shoe covers should be used particularly if the crime scene involves shoe impressions or deposits of body fluids or other materials that might be altered with the introduction of your own shoe prints or those of your fellow investigators.

20. Jumpsuit or coveralls made of cotton or other lint-free material to wear over—or instead of—your street clothing while at the crime scene.

21. Cord, rope, string, wire, wire ties, and packing tape.

22. Staplers, staples, thumbtacks, transparent tape, and paper clips for fastening and sealing objects and containers.

23. Bottle of alcohol and/or 15 percent bleach solution for washing hands and instruments such as knives, calipers, and other evidence-collecting devices.

24. Moist antibacterial towelettes, individually wrapped, for quick cleanup when soap and water are not immediately available. These convenient wipes can also be used for washing off tools and cutting instruments.

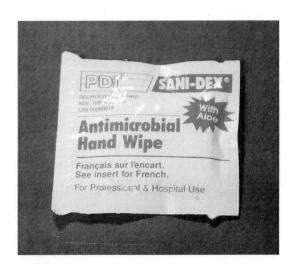

Figure 2.8   Antibacterial wipes are useful when disinfecting your hands after working with biohazardous evidence.

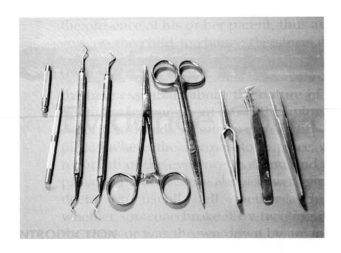

Figure 2.9 Dental and medical tools are excellent to have in a CSI kit to mark and collect evidence.

25. Paper towels and cleansing tissues.

26. Knife, scalpel, X-acto knife and blades, and scissors.

27. Mirrors, including a dental mirror for peering under and behind objects that cannot be moved, or inside hard-to-reach places.

28. Magnets for retrieving small metal objects from hard-to-reach places.

29. Tweezers and grabbing devices with long handles to pick up objects out of reach.

Figure 2.10 Different-size glass jars and vials are crucial in preserving small items of evidence, especially when they are in a liquid form.

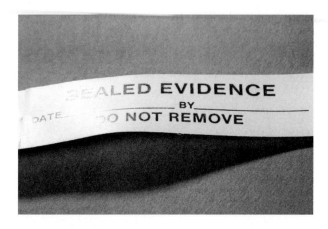

Figure 2.11   Evidence seals like this are placed on evidence bags, boxes, or even cars to help with the chain of custody.

30. Brushes of various shapes and sizes for sweeping and cleaning.

31. Syringes, pipettes, and turkey basters for collecting or dispensing liquids.

32. Glass vials, paper bags, plastic bags, canisters, bottles, boxes, and other containers for evidence.

33. Tapes and labels for securing evidence in containers and for identifying the evidence. Gummed labels may also be used for sealing some containers. A broken seal will indicate that the package had been opened or tampered with.

34. Cotton balls and Styrofoam "popcorn" for cushioning items in packing.

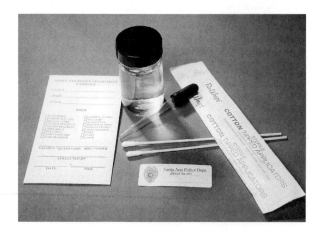

Figure 2.12   A blood collection kit should contain distilled water, sterile swabs, and proper identification labels.

Figure 2.13a A basic print kit should contain a brush, black powder in a wide-mouth jar, lifting tape in various widths, latent lift cards, and a pocket ink pad.

35. Sterile cotton swabs, weigh paper and swatches, and distilled water for lifting dried traces of blood and other traces from absorbent surfaces, such as concrete or asphalt.

36. Silicone, microsil, traxtone, and plaster casting materials, including rubber bowls for mixing the materials. Carry a couple gallons of bottled water in case tap water is not available at the scene.

37. Fingerprint powders, including magna powder, Super Glue (cyanoacrylate ester), and other materials for developing and lifting latent prints.

38. Report forms, cards, tags, envelopes, and paper to fold into bindles for powders that might be evidence.

Figure 2.13b When out on a scene where it may not be possible to collect the evidence, a portable fuming wand can be used to develop fingerprints with cyanoacrylate ester (Super Glue).

Figure 2.13c These finger-prints were developed on paper using black magna powder.

39. Vials with reagents provided by the lab for field tests of substances suspected of being blood, drugs, or other controlled substances.

40. Containers with saline and distilled-water solution for collecting and preserving substances, such as blood, semen, and other body fluids.

41. Water and nourishment items for your thirst and hunger in the event you are going to be on the scene for long periods of time with no breaks.

42. Magnifying glass and jeweler's loop for close-up examination of engravings, prints, trace evidence, and jewelry.

Figure 2.14 This loop is commonly used by fingerprint examiners when comparing unknown fingerprints to a set of known inked impressions.

43. Corrugated boxes and large paper grocery bags for transportation of large items of evidence or many separately packaged items to be packed in the larger containers for convenience in transporting and prevention of cross-contamination.

44. Metal scribe and engraving tool for marking items of evidence with your logo and other essential identifying data.

45. Self-sealing plastic bags for small items.

46. Evidence tape and tags for sealing and identifying evidence.

47. Printed routing forms for each item of evidence for initial identification and to document each step along the way in its continuity of custody.

SUMMARY

In this chapter we have attempted to make as complete a list as possible for your basic crime scene investigation kit. We suggest that you use it when putting your kit together, and when you prepare your inventory list.

SUGGESTED OUTSIDE PROJECTS

1. Visit your local police department and discuss the inventory list with the officer in charge of crime scene investigations. Make all the necessary corrections that will make the list more functional.

2. Draw up a list of items that should be included in a crime scene investigation van or truck. Visit a local department that has such a vehicle used solely for crime scene investigations. Compare how it is equipped with your list of how you believe such a vehicle should be equipped.

DISCUSSION QUESTIONS

1. Is there a better type of highway warning device than the old traditional railroad flare?

2. What is the advantage of using a steel ruler versus a cloth measuring tape?

3. To what extent, if any, is digital photography used in the police agencies in your neighborhood?

4. Describe a scenario in which it would be wise to use a camcorder for liability protection.

5. List and discuss any additional items that should be included in the list presented in this chapter.

6. Would you recommend placing a "North" arrow in each scene before taking each photograph at the crime scene? Why? Why not?

7. What is the technical name of Super Glue, and how is it used to develop fingerprints?

8. What information should an evidence card contain?

9. What is a "reagent," and for what type of substance would you use it?

10. What type of camera is best for crime scene photography?

Chapter Three
The Initial Response

INTRODUCTION

When you are assigned to proceed to the crime scene, whether you are the primary officer assigned to the case to investigate, or the specialist assigned to investigate only the crime scene, your responsibility enroute to the scene will be the same. That is to report to communications and to your colleagues what observations you make and whatever information comes your way. You may observe vehicles or people moving away from the scene or perhaps lingering in the area. On first sight, they mean nothing to you, but as the case develops those people or vehicles that you saw while you were enroute become significant. Be sure to include all observations in your reports and debriefing with other officers participating in the investigation.

It is your responsibility as part of the team to take advantage of all the help you can get from others, and to provide your share of help in return. The old saying "It's amazing how much good work gets done if it does not matter who gets the credit" applies to the crime investigation team. Your good work will be recognized through your reports and your successful presentation of evidence in the courtroom.

SUGGESTED PROCEDURE

1. *Acknowledge the call.* Wherever you are or whatever you are doing at the time of receiving the call, be sure to let the dispatcher and other field units know the location you are coming from and your estimated time of arrival. If it is a Code Three or Code Two call, you know that you will not be the only unit that responds. Other units that may not even be

assigned will be heading in that direction if they believe you might need help or they may spot a suspect fleeing from the scene. Other units responding to the same call and other emergency vehicles responding to other calls can plan their own routes of travel.

2. *Get the details available.* What is the nature of the crime as reported to the department? Is there any immediate danger to arriving officers? Is there a hostage situation? Are the suspects still at or near the scene? Are there any injuries to victims? What other help is on the way, such as paramedics, fire department, public works, or other? Are there any descriptions of fleeing suspects or vehicles? Do not wait to find out these details until you arrive at the scene, as you may be able to plan for your arrival if you have some of that information, if it is available.

3. *Request a description of the premises if you are not familiar with them.* There may be tricky access problems to that particular building or neighborhood, such as streets that are inaccessible or closed, such as under construction or congested because of media or emergency vehicles at the scene. The building may have roof access or doors through which you may choose for entry instead of the main entrance.

4. *Inventory your equipment.* This should be done before you leave the office, but if for some reason you did not, it may be wise to stop your vehicle for a minute before an emergency arises, and make a quick check to assure yourself that all the equipment and supplies you need are there, and to avoid the embarrassment of being unprepared. If your inventory turns up short and you do not have the time to go back to the office to pick up the necessary supplies, request a follow-up unit to bring the needed items to you at the scene.

5. *Visualize your arrival and plan of action.* While enroute to the scene, visualize the scene as reported to you and as you anticipate your assault upon the task. Mentally note how you are going to stake out the boundaries of the crime scene if officers on the scene have not done so already. Anticipate the presence of witnesses, onlookers, and representatives of the media who are going to interfere with your investigation, and how you are going to have them removed from the premises. After you arrive, you will, no doubt, have to change some of

Figure 3.1   Each officer who enters or leaves a scene should be logged in and out. That officer should also document his or her role or purpose at the scene.

your plans, but you will be mentally prepared to carry out that exercise. Always keep an open mind to all contingencies.

6. *Survey the scene as you arrive.* Look around for people and objects that your instinct tells you are out of place. After committing a crime of almost any category, the perpetrator may come back and hang around, watching the investigators at work. Just because a person is not running away from the scene does not mean that he or she is an innocent bystander. Lookouts for burglars may actually appear to be a couple of lovers "making out" in a car near the scene or the ice cream vendor with his pushcart or a lady walking her dog. In short, be suspicious of everyone and report your observations to the officer in charge of the investigation or who is serving as scribe. If something appears to be completely out of order, call for a follow-up unit to check it out.

7. *Communicate, communicate, communicate.* Keep in constant touch with the dispatcher and your fellow officers and keep them abreast of every aspect of the situation as it develops. This does not mean that you must keep up a running dialogue of inane gobbledygook. In addition to telling other officers in the area

about suspicious activities on the way, broadcast your arrival. Use a telephone or your radio to advise the dispatcher if all is under control or if you need more help or assistance. If there is more information on a suspect or vehicle that has left the scene, get that information out as soon as possible. If an arrest has been made and all is now under control, broadcast that information also. Call off the backup units that might have been necessary when the original call went out but are no longer needed.

8. *Assess the situation.* Determine the parameters of the crime scene and see that it is properly taped off and protected. If there are not enough officers to keep others away from the scene, consider using a witness to do the job, and then you will also be assured that he or she will still be around when witnesses are to be questioned. Confer with the other officers on the scene and make sure the workload is apportioned correctly and that everyone does his or her assigned job. One officer may be in charge of the overall investigation while you are responsible only for the crime scene investigation. In a homicide case, custody of the body and determination of cause of death is to be determined by the coroner, but you and your colleagues are responsible for investigating the crime. Cooperation among agencies is of prime importance.

9. *If you are the first to arrive, look after the safety of the participants.* Either administer first aid yourself or delegate a qualified person to handle that task. Personal life is more sacred than bits of evidence.

10. *Locate and separate witnesses.* An officer should be assigned to keep track of witnesses until the assigned investigator questions each one. If you are alone, consider putting the witnesses to work, such as keeping others away from the scene, directing traffic, administering first aid, and writing their statements on a notepad. Witnesses should be kept apart as much as possible because you want to get individual statements, not "jury statements" by the person with the stronger personality convincing the others that only his or her account of the events is the correct one.

11. *Determine the true nature and scope of the crime.* You do this by examining the scene, listening to the victims and witnesses, and making your own assessment in consultation with your

Figure 3.2 Wet shoe prints coming off of a wet grass area onto concrete are an example of transient evidence. These shoe prints will evaporate and must be photographed immediately before they disappear.

fellow officers on the scene. It is not unusual for people to make false crime reports for many different reasons, such as defrauding an insurer or causing trouble for an enemy.

12. *Locate and protect transient or short-lived evidence.* When weather conditions are less than ideal, you may have to take care to preserve this type of evidence before you do anything else, because any delay may result in the loss of the evidence. For example, a wet shoe print on a dry tile floor will soon dry and disappear. What appears to be a spilled liquid may actually be blood or some other body fluid that needs collection and analysis but may be wiped up by a fastidious housekeeper.

13. *Begin your systematic search for evidence.* Chapter Four is devoted to this subject. We will cover that in greater detail later.

14. *Allow nonessential people to enter the scene only after you release it when your investigation is complete.* You are in charge of the crime scene. Once you release the scene, you will never be able to go back and re-create the scene exactly as it was. People clean, move, and remove things from the premises, sometimes changing the scene completely to help them forget the undesirable experience of the crime. Even in the event that you do go back to the scene after you have released it, and upon your return you find crucial evidence, how are you going to prove that it was not put there after your investigation rather than preceding it?

SUMMARY

Accepting the assignment to investigate the crime scene and getting to that scene quickly and safely are crucial to the success of the investigation. But your responsibility as a part of the investigative team is to work with the other investigators as a team member, observing and reporting everything that comes to your attention that may help in solving the case. In this chapter, we have gone through a step-by-step procedure of what to do from the time you first receive the call to go to the scene until you have arrived and begun your part of the investigation.

SUGGESTED OUTSIDE PROJECTS

1. Set up a ride-along with a crime scene investigation officer in your local police or sheriff's department. If possible, make two or three separate tours lasting a full eight- or ten-hour shift each. Write a report on your observations and include an evaluation of the work performance of the officers involved.

2. Write an essay on how officers can mess up a crime scene investigation by not following the prescribed procedures. An example might be that one of the witnesses is actually the suspect who returned to the scene as the officers arrived, but was able to give faulty information to the officers and mislead their investigation. In this example, an officer who had observed that person arrive after the officers arrived failed to give that information to the officers taking the report.

DISCUSSION QUESTIONS

1. When you are out in the field, how should you communicate acknowledgment of the assignment to investigate a crime scene?

2. Is it possible that a reported burglary might prove to have been no crime at all?

3. What value would a plot map of the area surrounding the crime scene have for the responding officers to the crime scene?

4. For a business burglary call, how would blueprints of the building help you when you respond to a call to investigate the crime?

5. Why do you believe that the authors emphasized item seven on the list by writing *communicate* three times?

6. If you had the opportunity of saving the life of a critically injured victim, but it would mean destroying critical evidence, what would you do?

7. Why should witnesses be separated before giving their statements?

8. Describe three different types of short-lived or transient evidence, and explain why it is so important to identify and handle such evidence early in your investigation.

9. How would you mark off a crime scene if it were a robbery inside a convenience market?

10. What would you add to the list presented in this chapter?

Chapter Four
The Crime Scene Search

INTRODUCTION

Whatever you are searching for, you must do it systematically and thoroughly. Additionally, when you are searching a crime scene and many onlookers are nearby, you must appear to know what you are doing. If you carry out your search in a haphazard and careless manner, you will cause irreparable damage to your reputation and that of your department. A sloppy search indicates that the searcher is probably sloppy in everything he or she does.

The community policing programs that involve your department and the public have a very positive effect in that the public is more involved, but a cautionary note is that those people are watching their officers more carefully, and they are more likely to recognize sloppy police work. The ubiquitous media, especially those presenting "breaking news," will be nearby to record your activity for posterity, and many armchair detectives will critique your work every time your act is shown on local news programs. A word of advice: Be thorough and be professional.

PLAN YOUR SEARCH

All searches require that you proceed according to an organized and coordinated plan. There are different kinds of searches, depending on what you are looking for, such as searches for people (missing and lost children and adults, and suspects of all ages and genders) and searches for objects. You may be searching the premises where a burglar has taken away stolen objects and left behind evidence. You may be searching an office building for bombs purported to having been planted on the premises. In all searches you are looking for evidence of all types. Planning is your key to greater success in finding what you are looking for, as well as many items you had no idea you would find. Whether you work alone or with other searchers, draw a plan on paper and apportion the search so that each area is searched at least twice, and each time by a different person. Draw your search plan, assign searchers, and check off each area when the search is complete. If curious onlookers are nearby, post a guard to watch the searched areas to prevent contamination or evidence planting.

INTERIOR SEARCHES

Try to arrange for optimum lighting conditions, utilizing available lights at the scene, bringing in more flood lamps with portable generators, and using your battery-operated flashlights as well. If you are searching a building where the electricity is off, your only available lighting will probably be your flashlights and portable floods. Under these conditions, when you move from a lighted area where your eyes are conditioned to the light into a dark room or area, stop for a few seconds when you enter the dark and let your eyes adjust to the light change. The rods and cones of the eyes reverse functions when going from dark to light and vice versa, and the more dramatic the change, the longer the transition time.

Wear gloves for your search. If you believe there is a possibility of a suspect still being on the premises, you may choose to move with your weapon to a ready position. In those situations it is also wise to open each door by slamming it open until it strikes the wall or doorstop. If you hear a loud "Ugh" when you slam the door open, you have probably located a suspect hiding behind that door. In most crime scene searches, you or your colleagues have probably already cleared the area of any suspects so it will not be necessary to move with a weapon in your hand or to slam doors open. You have now moved on to the evidence search phase of the investigation.

As you move from room to room or one section of the search to another, stop frequently and listen for sounds, try to identify odors, and absorb the atmosphere of the scene. Sounds such as air conditioning or heaters turning on and off, or the foundation settling, and odors such as perfume, cigar or pipe smoke, and aftershave lotion may prove valuable to your investigation later. For example, a person confessing to the crime may at some time state that the air conditioner was on full blast and made him shiver. As for odors, you may recognize the odors on the suspect's person as being similar to those you smelled earlier during your crime scene search.

Take Polaroid photos or start videorecording the scene as you enter and move around the scene to get an overall view before you start your intensive search. If you have neither a Polaroid nor a camcorder, use a voice-actuated tape recorder or make good mental notes. These will be your initial observations. You will later begin using your 35mm SLR camera for the more detailed evidence photos that we will cover in Chapter Nine. If you have a notepad in hand, make a rough sketch of the crime scene and the general area for orientation purposes. You will prepare more detailed sketches later. These photos and rough sketches may help you reconstruct the scene in your mind when you are preparing your reports, and sometimes the initial photos may show certain items that may not show up later in your more detailed photographs. It may lead you to discover that someone has possibly contaminated the scene or just inadvertently moved something. In the celebrated Jeffrey McDonald murder case several years ago it was revealed that one of the ambulance drivers picked up and pocketed an item at the scene, believed to be a wallet belonging to McDonald.

Even though you are wearing gloves, touch nothing that you believe might bear trace evidence until you are sure that touching will not wipe away fingerprints or other traces. Shine a light obliquely across the surface over the floor and other flat surfaces before you walk on them to search for footprints or shoe prints in the dust that has settled since the last time the surface was dusted. Use the oblique light procedure over all surfaces that might have been disturbed. Sometimes undisturbed dust may yield information also. For example, one of the authors was taking a burglary report from an auto parts shop owner, who listed dozens of items that had been stolen, but about a month's accumulation of dust on the shelves where the victim claimed the merchandise had been stored was not disturbed. When it was pointed out to the victim that if merchandise had been on those shelves the merchandise and not the shelves would be covered with dust. The owner then admitted he was "padding" the report a little for his insurance claim. It is reasonable to assume that he probably dusted his shelves more frequently after that.

Divide the room or area into halves or quadrants, depending on the number of people you have involved in the search, and assign individuals or teams to each section. Next, divide the room into levels at which the search will be performed, such as one-third of the wall from the floor up, then the second one-third, and finally the rest of the way to the ceiling, followed by the spaces above the ceiling or false ceiling and crawl hole. Later, when each officer or team of officers has completed their part of the search, switch searchers and repeat the process. It is not unusual for one person to miss something that another person will find. As you know, sometimes we have blind spots where we look at something yet do not see it. Has it ever happened to you that a close friend comes within your visual range at a conference, for example, and you didn't see that person until perhaps a half hour later, and your excuse was "I didn't see you come in"? In the more serious crimes, a secondary search should be considered mandatory, and preferably at a time when the lighting conditions are at an optimum level.

Ceiling Area

Look for false ceilings, and search the area between that structure and the real ceiling, and the attic where there are accessible crawl spaces. Burglars have been known to climb up into crawl holes that one would not imagine could bear such weight and bulk. The moral here is to search even the most illogical places for people and contraband, so your search is truly more thorough than if you were to search only the obvious places. Search inside the ceiling light fixtures and ducts for air conditioning, ventilation, and heating systems. Sound or speaker systems, power conduits, or other pipes and enclosed areas should be given meticulous attention. Look behind and inside moldings and frames if they are loose or appear to have been disturbed. Search any façade or other object that appears to be part of the room design but might be hollow and hide contraband.

Windows and Door Frames

Look for access points to hollow cores of doors and framing that have been disturbed or that could possibly conceal small hidden items, such as bindles of drugs or folded paper. Curtain and drape rods are good hiding places.

Walls

The spaces between walls are extremely good as hiding places. Sometimes a false wall will conceal an entire room that has been sealed off with plaster and wallboard. If you think there might be such a hidden room, take outside measurements of the structure and compare that with inside measurements. You may discover an unexplained difference of several feet, which could well be a sealed closet space that has been designated as a hiding space, which is perhaps accessible from the attic or a crawl hole in the ceiling of the basement. Switch plates and plug plates and spaces behind photos and other wall hangings provide access to the walls. Merely tapping on the wall will produce a hollow sound because most walls are hollow. Look around the edges of the wall, such as at the ceiling and floor and door and window frames. It may be necessary to tear out part of the wall in very critical searches.

Miscellaneous

Building plans and blueprints may reveal valuable information about the original structure compared with its current configuration. Doors, windows, and stairways may have been eliminated or covered over. In a recent case in Southern California, a newly poured patio floor was dug up by narcotics officers and revealed a cache of more than a million dollars in cash. Consider also the cold war scare when people built bomb shelters in their backyards or under their houses, which by now have fallen into disrepair and may have been closed up and forgotten.

Insulation materials serve as excellent camouflage. Recently hung wallpaper on only one wall, which looked like a sloppy job at that, revealed a very valuable stolen painting hidden under the wallpaper. Move bookcases and other pieces of furniture that are placed against hidden wall openings, over floor openings, or covering damaged or stained carpeting. You will then conduct detailed searches of the furniture, inside and under drawers, spaces behind drawers, inside and under mattresses, even hollow spaces under waterbeds. The possibilities are endless.

Search Warrant Searches

When you are acting on a search warrant, your search will be limited to searching only those places described in the warrant, and only for items that have been listed as possible or probable in those places consistent with the search. You don't look into dresser drawers for stolen auto tires and wheels. However, if your search is consistent with what you hope to find and you come across other items that you believe to be contraband, guard the "treasure" against destruction or concealment and secure a new warrant to search for more contraband of the nature of your new discovery. As you have learned in the academy and in your criminal procedures classes, a search warrant is not a hunting or fishing license, and it has many restrictions.

Floors

Check the floor carefully for any loose boards, recently installed tiles or carpeting, or recent repair work to the floor or its covering. Color differences of floor covering may indicate that stains have been removed. You may search any area that might have contained bloodstains with tests that are described in Chapter Five. In a murder case several years ago, the murderer decided to break up with his girlfriend. When she objected to such an abrupt end to their relationship, he acceded to a final fling, but he wanted it to be a threesome with another woman participating. The other woman had been a mutual friend or perhaps his previous girlfriend. They had their ménage à trois with the second woman videotaping a sex act between the two who were breaking up, during which the man tortured and murdered the woman. This was all on tape. Afterward, the videographer handed the tape to the killer and went home. Some time later, the killer was questioned about the disappearance of his former girlfriend, then eventually arrested and prosecuted for her murder. The third party in the sex scene who took the pictures testified to what had happened that fateful night and told about the tape. The police could not find the tape and relied only on that witness's account of the murder. The defendant testified that he was innocent and knew nothing of his former lover's whereabouts. The defense then brought up enough evidence of alcoholism and mental instability of the prosecution's star witness that the jury voted for acquittal of the murderer.

A couple of years after the murder, the freed killer, who had already been in jeopardy and found not guilty, sold his house where the murder had occurred. The new owners decided to remodel, and when they started tearing up flooring and repairing holes in the walls they found the missing tape. They played it on their VCR, saw the murder take place on the tape, and turned the tape over to the FBI, who turned it over to the local prosecuting attorney. Because the killer had already been declared not guilty, he could not be tried again for the murder due to the double jeopardy rule of the Fifth Amendment. But, because he had testified during his trial that he knew nothing of the murder, he was prosecuted and convicted for perjury. It was no consolation to the victim's survivors, but the man did serve a few years in prison and partially paid for his crime. All this because the officers who searched the premises missed a most valuable piece of evidence: the tape.

EXTERIOR SEARCHES

Once you and your colleagues have established the parameters of the crime scene and search areas, divide each area into workable portions and delegate each subarea to yourself and your colleagues, who are working either solo or in teams of two. If you are conducting the search all by yourself, sketch out the entire area, break it into workable subareas, then search one subarea at a time, checking off on your sketch each part of the search area as you complete that part of the search.

You may choose to use any method you believe best for each individual search, such as a spiral, quadrants, ever-expanding or contracting circles, or back and forth in a straight line in a pattern as one follows when mowing a lawn. What you call it is of lesser importance than how thoroughly you conduct your search. Even when you are working alone, go back and search again, changing your method so as to maximize the chances of finding something you might have missed the first time. You not only must be efficient but also must present the image that you know what you are doing. This is true especially when you have people watching you work, such as that news photographer in a tree nearby, or some Monday morning quarterback who will tell everyone within earshot how sloppy you were when looking for evidence. It may sound a little paranoid, but believe us, what you do and how you do your job reflect on other people's assessment of your department. You do not want your operation to be called a "cesspool of incompetence." In other words, you must not only know what you are doing, but you must *appear* as though you know what you are doing.

If the weather is working against you, such as rain, snow, or high winds, you are probably going to change the sequence of your investigation so that you may search for those items that are most likely to be destroyed or altered. Shoe prints in a mud puddle or pools of blood that will be washed away unless collected immediately, will take precedence over evidence that can wait until you have taken care of the short-lived evidence. If you are conducting your search on a street, a highway, or a heavily traveled sidewalk during rush hour, you will want to plan your search so that your investigation will not suffer, yet will get the traffic moving as soon as possible.

There is no sense or reason where people choose hiding places. For that reason you must expect to find people and objects where one would *least likely* find them. Desperate people can fit into places so small that it takes the fire department and its jaws of life to get them out. People have been found in trash compactors (a nine-year-old boy), air-conditioning and heating ducts, chimneys, kitchen and bathroom cabinets, even desk or dresser drawers. Even when you are looking for larger items, consider that the person who hid them has possibly dismantled them and hidden their parts in several places. A postal inspector once told the story that a soldier during the Korean War sent a souvenir of an enemy's confiscated gun home, but not all in one piece. As the story goes, an alert postal clerk discovered a single piece of a gun in his first letter, and each succeeding letter contained another piece of the gun. When the soldier sent the last piece, the postal inspector put all the separate pieces together and reconstructed the whole gun. He then charged the soldier with sending a firearm through the mails. Even though the story sounds a little "fishy," it does make the point that people do ingenious things to skirt the law.

If it does not complicate your investigation, have someone familiar with the place to be searched, possibly an employee or tenant, accompany you while you search for items that are missing or that have been left behind by the perpetrator. Be cautious when listening to claims about certain items stolen or moved, and do not accept at face value every word that person tells you. He or she may have a secret agenda, which might include misleading the investigation or exaggerating his or her losses to defraud the insurer. Some people pay burglars and thieves to steal their cars or merchandise so that they can collect the insurance and split their earnings with the people who allegedly victimized them.

Search for Bombs

Searches for suspected bombs, such as a phoned-in bomb threat, should be left to the specialists who are trained and equipped for such searches. But, as a crime scene investigator, you may find yourself the first one on the scene and searching for suspicious objects until the bomb squad arrives. Be careful to leave in place any object that you suspect might be a bomb, evacuate the area, and stand by until the experts arrive. If the suspected object is in a building, evacuate the entire building. If you do conduct such a preliminary search, take along someone who is familiar with the building and its content to advise you of objects disturbed or perhaps a package left on the premises that was not there earlier. Parcel deliveries, including packages that arrived by a postal carrier, should be handled as though they were bombs until the bomb squad has cleared them.

When searching for a bomb or similar device, do not use any radio equipment, turn on or off any light switches, or operate any device that might spark and set off a device of some sort. Do not allow anyone to smoke, and avoid inserting and pulling out electric plugs. Some explosive devices have spring-wound clocks for timing and may be heard ticking if you are searching in absolute silence. If and when you find what you recognize as a bomb, or what you suspect might be a bomb, and you have verified that the bomb squad is on its way to the scene, withdraw from the area and make sure the surrounding area has been evacuated. After the bomb has been removed and/or neutralized, then continue your crime scene search.

The Search Continues

If practical, put plastic covers over your shoes and wear gloves to avoid leaving impressions of your own at the scene, and continue your search. We have conveniently forgotten the name of the author, but one writer of an investigation text recommends that you keep your hands in your pockets while searching a crime scene. This is neither wise nor practical, as evidence can be collected only by moving and collecting things. Your responsibility is to determine if a crime has, in fact, been committed and to conduct a thorough investigation. Keep an open mind throughout the entire time you are on the premises, and avoid forming any preconceived notions about the outcome of your search. If you have a fixed objective, you may find only what you expect to find during your search. Sometimes claims made by crime victims may not be borne out by the facts. If your investigation is thorough, the evidence will speak for itself and either verify or disprove the statements made by the victims.

As you continue the process of investigating, stop occasionally and conceptualize the crime as it might have happened. What would be the likely point of entry? Exit? What route of travel did the perpetrator(s) take while committing the crime? Imagine that you are in the perpetrator's shoes and how you would have carried out the action. Consider the timing. How much can be accomplished in the time "window" when the crime must have occurred? For example, in an armed robbery of a gold vault, the two owners of the company stated that they were held up at gunpoint and tied up. Then several million dollars' worth of gold bricks were removed from the vault in twenty minutes by two men who used a three-quarter-ton pickup truck to cart away the loot. Gold is heavy, as the officers knew. All they did was to add up the tons of gold that had allegedly been stolen, then estimated that a pickup truck of that size would have to make several trips and a couple of hours to cart all that gold away. After pointing this out to the victims when questioning them separately, one of the victims confessed that actually they had only about a half dozen bricks in all in their vault, which they showed to the owners who wanted to look at their gold. They used the same gold bricks to show all the people and did not expect anyone to take their gold out of the vault because gold has to be assayed and weighed each time it is moved. Handling gold causes small particles to be scraped off with fingernails or by such objects as rings or bracelets, and consequently reduces its value. The two vault owners panicked when they received a surprise notification from one of their customers, who became suspicious of their activities and told them that he had gone to the police to investigate what he believed to be a major scam. They feared that the police would come with a search warrant and find that they had been selling the same few gold bricks many times over. The vault owners were subsequently convicted for major felony fraud, and the misdemeanor charge of filing a false police report was dropped.

In order to avoid allegations of incompetence or dishonesty, be sure to document your search very carefully with accurate notes, photographs, and fellow officers paying attention to each other throughout the investigation. Do not overlook the possibility of using a videographer for the express purpose of liability protection, as covered earlier. You will want to document discrepancies between what victims and witnesses describe happened and what did or did not happen. For example, a witness may distinctly remember having seen the culprit crawl in through the window. When you examine the window, you will see that the glass has been broken, and jagged pieces of the glass still sticking up in the frame, but no blood or snagged clothing on the jagged edges of the glass or on the windowsill, which would surely be there if someone had crawled through that window. Your photos or video will show this discrepancy without your having to editorialize that the reporting party has probably lied.

Sometimes a so-called "victim" will try to convince you that a window was broken from the outside and entry was made through that window. Your investigation shows that the window was broken from the inside, because it had been raining during the past few hours, there are no muddy footprints in the flowerbed below the window, and no muddy scuff marks on the outside wall, which would have been placed there by a person climbing in through the window.

It is not unusual for a bona fide crime to be enhanced by victims who magnify their losses either intentionally or unintentionally. Under extreme emotional stress, three assailants may appear as five, or a man, who is five foot, three inches, may seem to be much taller and heavier. Some victims are embarrassed to say that they were beat up by someone smaller and who might appear weaker than they are. Some victims exaggerate their

Figure 4.1 Documentation and notes are crucial during the course of your crime scene investigation.

losses so that the insurance will pay them for their entire loss and also cover their deductible amount, or to replace worn-out or lost tools that they would rather the insurance company buy for them. Other victims make simple errors in describing the event and calculating their losses.

RECORDING THE SEARCH

We have already mentioned the use of recording devices, such as a tape recorder, video camcorder, Polaroid, and other cameras. When your investigation team is large enough, one of the members of the team should be the scribe. Otherwise, you are the scribe along with your other duties. Every action taken by the team members should be written down exactly as it happens, and whenever a discovery of some new information or evidence is made, the scribe should record the time, exact location, description of the find, and precisely who made the discovery.

The scribe should also keep a log to record arrivals and departures of all persons at the scene for any reason whatsoever. If a supervisor just drops by at 8:47 A.M. to check on the progress of the investigation, the time and name of that supervisor should be entered on the log. You should take photos of their shoes or their fingerprints if they have touched anything during their visit to the scene. Include all persons because some time later it may be discovered that one of those people may have left shoe impressions at the scene.

The scribe's log will be incorporated into the completed package of reports. Some crime reports and supplemental reports add up to thousands of pages before the case finally goes to court. In addition to the scribe's log, each participant involved in the investigation will be required to complete an individual report with a complete account of exactly what he or she did, and might have found, and all the details of his or her participation. The officer assigned as principal investigator of the case will have the responsibility of collecting and coordinating all of those reports, and putting them together so that they will have continuity and clarity for those who will read them. All participants should later read through the reports of their individual action to check for the accuracy of their contribution.

TRANSIENT OR SHORT-LIVED EVIDENCE

Be careful to identify and protect transient evidence that is not likely to last long because of the weather conditions, such as rain or snow or warming sunlight, or because of vehicular or foot traffic that is likely to destroy the evidence if it is not addressed immediately. Skid marks on a heavily traveled roadway will soon blend in with previous and subsequent skid marks and may not be distinguishable from each other. Shoe or foot impressions in dust will blow away with the next strong gust of wind. Wet prints on a dry floor will dry as the sun rises. The wet marks should be noted and sketched, and photographed when first observed, or they will be lost forever. In the rain, muddy shoe prints might wash away. Sometimes you run across the well-meaning person who will start cleaning up the mess at the scene even before you have completed your investigation. It is not unusual for sex crime victims to destroy the evidence of the attack on their own bodies by bathing or douching, and putting stained bedclothes in the washing machine. These victims are probably not even thinking of the harm they are causing to your investigation because of their personal emotional trauma.

These items of transient evidence may not prove to be your most crucial evidence, but when you are searching the scene and collecting all available evidence, you may not be in a position to know which items of evidence are best and which are not. Meticulously and completely collect all items that are, or that might be, evidence, and then the evidence itself will often tell you what role it will play in your case.

CONDITIONS RELATED TO THE CRIME

Although they may not be counted as evidence, certain circumstances may help you determine the nature of the crime, the time of day, and perhaps something personal about the perpetrator, such as taste in food or preferences in radio or television shows. Here are some of the things you should be aware of while conducting your search.

1. Discarded candy and gum wrappers, cigarette and cigar butts or ashes, sales slips and receipts that might have fallen out of the perpetrator's pockets during the crime event.

2. Doors that are locked or unlocked, which are different than how the occupant left them before the crime.

3. Is there evidence of damage or destruction of the door or the lock that would indicate a forcible entry?

4. If doors or windows were damaged, was the damage done from the inside or the outside? This may indicate whether it is a point of exit or entry.

5. Was entry made with use of a key? Follow-up investigators will find out who had keys.

6. Is there evidence that a lock was picked, as indicated by metal shavings and broken pieces of a lock pick?

7. Are there small pieces of metal on the premises, possibly from a tool that the perpetrator took away from the scene?

8. Are the windows open or closed? Is the weather outside consistent with this? On a cold day, and usually at night for security reasons, the windows are closed and locked by the occupants.

9. Are the shades or drapes open or closed? Their position may indicate that the people inside like dark interiors during the daytime or that it was nighttime and the window coverings were closed for privacy. Some nudists and other people who are allergic to sunlight keep their windows covered day and night. Some burglars close the blinds and shades so that they may work where people outside cannot see them.

10. If a window or door glass has been broken and the debris on the sill and surrounding area is undisturbed, you may surmise that nobody could have gone through that opening without cutting himself or herself and/or disturbing the debris.

11. Are the lights on or off? Which lights may indicate whether a person went into the kitchen or used the bathroom? Status of the lights may also give you a clue as to whether the crime was committed during the day or night.

12. Specific lighting during any time of the day might indicate what the victim was doing at the time of the crime, such as working at a desk with the desk light on. This also might indicate that a thief might have turned on a desk light so as to see better when rifling through the desk drawers. Something like this might indicate that the perpetrator knew the location of his or her objective, which might point suspicion toward someone familiar with the premises.

13. What is the status of the heating and air conditioning? Some systems are designed to keep the ambient temperature constant, alternating heat and air, but most are set at one position

or the other. Air conditioning on at full blast might indicate that the occupants last touched the controls during the heat of the day, or at night. Some burglars like to work in comfort and may have set the controls themselves.

14. How about the food preparation areas in the kitchen? What meal was the last one eaten or prepared by the occupants? Are there dishes and cups left in the same condition as they were seen last by the victims? Perhaps the perpetrator(s) had a bite to eat to sustain themselves during their exploits. Check the kitchen sink and dishwasher for their contents to see if you get any hints about the modus operandi or identity of the culprits.

15. Is there an indication that perhaps guests were expected or had arrived, and were the guests possibly involved in the crime? Do the number of place settings equal the number of residents? This is especially important information to have if the residents have been murdered.

16. Can you detect any identifiable odors, such as perfumes, tobacco smoke, or medications, such as mentholated chest rub, and other substances that are foreign to this particular place of business or residence?

17. Check the sinks in the kitchen, bathrooms, and laundry room if you have a blood-related crime, such as a homicide or assault. Sometimes the assailant might attempt to wash blood off of tools or weapons. Even though the sink may appear to be clean, the elbow-shaped trap beneath the sink may contain valuable evidence because the perpetrator did not let the water run long enough to clear the pipes.

18. A toilet that has not been flushed completely may yield such evidence as cigarette butts or human waste deposited by the perpetrator, which may lead to determination of blood type or DNA of the perpetrator.

19. What is the condition of the bedding in the bedrooms? In sexual attack cases, you will collect all bedding to search for the presence of body fluids, hairs and fibers, and other evidence to substantiate the charges.

20. What is the state of dress or undress of the victims of assault or homicide victims? A rape suspect, for example, may claim that the sex was consensual, while the torn clothing of the victim may prove that extreme force was used.

21. Look at clocks and watches around the premises, and on those worn by the victims and suspects. A wall plug may have been pulled loose during the commission of a crime, or the time showing on a watch worn by a witness may be incorrect, and statements made may be crucially connected to his or her reference to the time on that watch or clock.

22. The "star 69" feature on a telephone will possibly call the phone number of the last party who called the residence or business where the crime occurred. Or you may choose to press the "redial" button to find out if the intruder made at least one phone call while on the premises and to whom that call was made.

23. If a cellular phone or pager was stolen in the crime, call the number of that unit and find out if anyone answers. Lost units are also found that way by calling the number and hearing the ring or buzz and leading you to its location. A car theft victim called the cell phone in his car. The person who answered was a friend of the car thief who was sitting in the car waiting for his friend to get out of class. A brief conversation led the victim and the local police to a high school in another city, where the car thief was arrested and the car recovered without damage.

24. Small areas, such as stairways, foyers, and hallways, may reveal items that have dropped out of an intruder's pockets. Have you sometimes taken your car keys out of your pocket and accidentally also removed coins or some other items at the same time?

25. Was the place ransacked by a person who was looking for anything of value, or did the intruder know exactly what he or she was looking for? This may identify the culprit as a member or friend of the family instead of a stranger.

26. Ask your tour guide through the crime scene, if you have one, if there is anything at all out of the ordinary, supporting our theory of transference.

SUMMARY

The search is one of the most important parts of any crime investigation. No matter how hard you try to do it better later, the first time you search must be your best and may be the only chance to conduct a full search. Missed evidence and crucial bits of data will be lost forever because of deliberate or accidental efforts of the occupants of the premises, whether interior or exterior, to clean up after the crime. Victims will have to clean up before resuming their lives at that location, and for them the sooner the better. Outside, many things will be changed by gardeners and cleanup crews for the resumption of normalcy, whatever that might be.

Be precise and thorough in your search, and keep an open mind. If you are looking for whatever may present itself to you, you are more likely to find it than if you have a preconceived idea about what you are going to find. It is sort of like saying: "If only I have two good pieces of evidence I can solve this case." You find the two items you were looking for, then stop. That is certainly no way to conduct an investigation. You can never collect too much evidence. Let the facts tell you what happened rather than shaping the facts to fit your hypothesis.

SUGGESTED OUTSIDE PROJECTS

1. Discuss this chapter with an experienced crime scene investigation specialist from your local police department. Get his views on what we have written here. Then, rewrite the chapter, as you believe it should have been written.

2. With your fellow students, set up an imaginary crime scene and hide at least eight items, which you designate as evidence. Give a list of those items to the team of students who are going to search and see if they find them all. Switch teams and repeat until all have had a chance to do their own search.

DISCUSSION QUESTIONS

1. When you are entering a room or area that is darker than the one you are leaving, what do the authors suggest that you do before you enter the new place?

2. Why slam a door open all the way to the doorstop before entering a room?

3. What is the primary purpose for wearing gloves and shoe covers when conducting a crime scene search?

4. What is *transient* evidence? Give an example of transient evidence.

5. Give a couple of examples of how you might suspect that a victim is exaggerating his or her loss.

6. What are the advantages of having two officers search a crime scene as a team?

7. Why would you have a second search by a different team if the first one were as thorough as it should be?

8. What is the function of a scribe?

9. Describe three or four different patterns of search when you are searching a room in which a crime occurred.

10. What should you do if you come across an object you believe to be a bomb while you are searching an office on the tenth floor of a building?

Chapter Five
Evidence Collection

INTRODUCTION

When you are searching for evidence, you may ask: "What is evidence?" That is an excellent question to start out this chapter. The answer is not quite so simple. There are actually two answers, one practical and the other academic. The practical answer is that we don't really know what is and is not evidence in a case until after we have collected every available item and bit of information that relates to a case, then analyzed everything and presented it to the prosecuting attorney. The attorney who is going to prosecute the case is the one who determines what is and is not evidence for this specific case, what is not relevant or material to the case, and what witness is not competent to testify for one reason or another. The academic definition is "Any species of proof, or probative matter, legally presented at the trial of an issue, by the act of the parties and through the medium of witnesses, records, documents, concrete objects, and so on. for the purpose of inducing belief in the minds of the court or jury as to their contention." Not only must the judge admit the evidence into the trial if it meets the tests of legality and constitutionality, but in the end the jury must accept it as proving a fact.

It is important to note the words *legally presented* in this definition. There are state and federal rules of evidence and constitutional safeguards protecting the residents and guests of this country against unreasonable violations of their personal and property privacy, and their right not to bear witness against themselves. In order to be able to legally present evidence you have collected, you must also show through testimony and documentation that there was a constant chain of custody from the time it was first discovered until it is presented in court.

In this chapter, we will list and discuss some of the many types of physical evidence you might find at the crime scene; how to collect, preserve, and transport them to the laboratory or evidence locker; and how they might help prove your case.

TIRE IMPRESSIONS

Tire manufacturers design and patent the treads on their products in distinctive patterns, which are exclusive to their brands only. A Goodyear tire tread will never look like that of a Bridgestone or a Winston tire tread, and vice versa. Many large laboratories, particularly those of the Federal Bureau of Investigation and many of the state laboratories, maintain files on tire patterns that are up to the current year and go back many years.

To collect tire impressions for evidentiary purposes, locate them on your sketch, indicating the length of each one and number or letter them in sequence if there is more than one impression. Next, photograph the impressions from an angle where you can include all impressions in the one photo, if there are more than one, and depicting their entire lengths. Take a series of photos of each impression from end to end, including a ruler in the photo so that you may enlarge each photo 1 to 1 (actual sizes) and so that the photos may be placed side by side to show the entire length of the impression.

When you locate a vehicle that holds the tires that you believe made the impressions in question, remove the wheels and roll their prints. To accomplish this task, you will want to have impressions of the entire circumference of each tire in question. Using butcher paper or newsprint approximately ten feet long, printers' ink, and a roller, roll ink on the tire tread all the way around where "the rubber meets the road," to paraphrase an old saying. Then roll the entire circumference of the tire onto the paper as you would roll a fingerprint. Compare this examplar of the suspected tire with the photographs and casts taken at the crime scene.

SHOE, BOOT, AND FOOTPRINTS

Shoe manufacturers, especially the ones that produce higher-quality products, place distinctive designs and logos on the heels and soles of their shoes and boots. In some cases you will find that even the heel and toe patterns are different than all others. From the impression you find in pliable material, such as mud or wax, you may find the patterns we mention, plus distinctive wear patterns, cuts, bruise marks, and imperfections that are unique to only one garment and its owner. You may determine the

Figure 5.1   Courtesy of County Sheriff's Office, Penobscot County, Maine.

approximate size of the shoe or boot, but in pliable material and under variable weather conditions it will probably not be possible to discern exact sizes. However, if the impression looks like a size 14, you can be sure that not many people wear size 14.

Footprints will also reveal the approximate size of shoe that person would wear, and there may be something unique about the shape of the foot or configuration of the toes that would aid in identifying the person who left the prints. People who are heavy or who carry heavy loads tend to make deeper impressions with their heels, and people who are running or walking fast will be lighter on their heels than their toes. The stride pattern will show a taller person and/or one who is running and taking longer strides than if walking. The stride pattern also will have a pattern. Watch runway models in a fashion show. You will notice that for the greatest effect to show off their fashions, they walk by taking each step directly in front of the other instead of forward and side by side, as does the average walker. Size and stride patterns of the impressions may give you a hint as to the age and gender of the person who made the impression, females and younger persons making smaller impressions and closer stride patterns than males and older persons.

People trained in the military service are likely to lead off by stepping first each time with the same foot, either right or left. A person walking with a limp will make a deeper impression with the stronger foot that bears the greater weight, and a cane or crutches may also leave an impression.

Figure 5.2   This partial shoe print impression was removed from a countertop using an electrostatic dust print lifter.

Measure the impressions and sketch them before taking photographs of individual impressions, the entire series of impressions, if any, and photos showing the stride pattern. Casting will be covered in a separate chapter.

When shoe, boot, and footprints are left on dusty surfaces, or wet prints are left on dry surfaces, you may be able to sketch and photograph only, except that you may find footprints made by shoeless persons that display patterns of the friction ridges. These can be dusted, lifted, and compared the same as palm and fingerprints. The experts may testify about footprints matching with the same authority as fingerprints. As for boots and shoes, the FBI and many other laboratories keep up-to-date files on logos, designs, and patterns of as many manufacturers' boots and shoes that they can find, and keep adding to their files as often as possible.

BLOOD AND BLOODSTAINS

Whenever you have a personal crime, such as rape, assault, criminal homicide, or kidnapping, you are likely to find blood and bloodstains at or near the scene. It is not unusual to find blood also at property crimes. The perpetrator may have injured himself or herself while entering the place, or while prying open containers or moving objects around, or perhaps by having a nosebleed as a result of extreme emotional pressure or bumping up against a hard object. Wherever you find broken glass or sharp objects, you are likely to find blood or other body fluids. Some people urinate or defecate when they are under extreme emotional stress. In a series of burglaries investigated by one of the authors, we found feces on top of the bed in each master bedroom, deposited there by an adolescent neighbor who wanted to make a statement about being a misfit among the other kids on the block.

The first step when finding blood or stains is to photograph them in their place, undisturbed, and to place them in your rough sketch. You may wish to make a quick determination whether the substance is blood, which is usually determined visually and by its distinctive odor, and for some reason it may be important to determine whether it is animal or human. Using prepared vials of reagent, it is fast and easy to conduct these tests, although you will not usually bother with these determinations until later in the lab.

The quantity of blood may show how profusely a person has bled at the scene, and the degree to which it has coagulated may indicate how recently the blood was deposited at that location. The droplets of blood will show whether the bleeder was moving, in what direction, and perhaps whether the movement was fast or slow. A large drop followed by smaller droplets indicates that the person was moving in the direction pointed by the ever-diminishing size of the droplets, which makes the pattern look like

Figure 5.3 This illustration shows that as a droplet of blood hits a surface, it makes a teardrop shape and then slowly thins out. By understanding this effect, one can determine the direction of travel that the blood originated from.

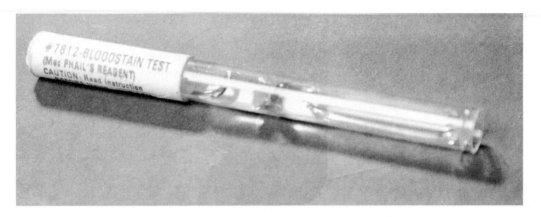

Figure 5.4 Bloodstain tests like this MacPhail's reagent are useful as a presumptive test to determine if a liquid or stain is in fact blood.

a tadpole. A thinner "tadpole-like" group of spots would indicate that the bleeder was moving faster than if the pattern looked like a fatter tadpole. The blood falling to the surface causes the splash pattern to point in the direction that the bleeder was moving. The spatter pattern may also lead an expert to testify as to an estimated height of the bleeder.

In addition to the reagents used to determine whether the substance is blood, which is usually a mixture including phenolpthalein or benzedine. Benzedine is seldom used since it has been determined to be a carcinogen. When the phenolpthalein is introduced to the substance believed to be blood, it will change color to a dark pink. Horseradish, potatoes, and other vegetables may also turn pink when mixed with the same reagent, but those foods are not likely to be confused with blood. The test is presumptive, not positive, but you may collect the substance with the expectation that it will test out as blood in the laboratory later.

Another test to determine the presence of blood on a surface when its presence is not readily visible is to spray a luminol reagent where you expect that you might find blood. In a dark room or area the luminol will make blood luminesce, therefore confirming your expectations of the presence of blood. This is particularly valuable when the floor or carpeting or upholstery has been washed or dry cleaned and the perpetrator believes he or she has destroyed all evidence of his or her crime. Blood will show up with luminol sometimes even after a car has been professionally detailed or the surface thoroughly cleaned (although not really), breaking down another defense claim that there was no bloodshed.

Now that you have photographed the blood drops and stains, and have verified that they are blood, your next step is to collect them.

Whenever possible, always strive to collect blood in its natural wet state, but if it is dry already, or for some reason you must let it dry before collecting it, be very careful to let it dry in a natural atmosphere. Avoid using such drying instruments as a hair dryer to speed up the process. That works well on hair but not on bloodstains.

When the blood is wet, your objective is to keep it in its liquid condition. Use a clean pipette and rubber bulb for suction, transferring the blood to a clean glass vial. If the blood appears to begin to congeal, drop a little drop of a saline solution onto the blood before drawing it up through the pipette. Your laboratory will provide you with the saline solution, but if you run out, you may make your own by mixing one teaspoonful of salt and one quart of distilled water. When you are not using it, keep the container tightly sealed to keep out contaminants. When you have collected as much of the wet blood as possible, seal the container and refrigerate it as soon as you can.

Collect partially dry bloodstains in two steps. First, collect the wet portion with a pipette and place it in a glass vial to keep it in its liquid state. Second, go to another task for a couple of minutes and let the blood dry completely. Then collect it as you take other dried blood samples. Be sure to label both the dry and wet portions of that sample to establish that they were from the same stain.

Collect dried blood by using either of two different methods. If the stain is on a nonporous surface, use a scalpel or X-acto knife to scrape as much of the entire stain as possible, placing the scrapings onto a dry square of clean paper that you will fold into a bindle to completely encase the material. You may use a clear plastic bag for the dried blood samples, but some of the material may get lost in the corners of the bag. The bindle has been used more traditionally. After you have scraped all the dried blood off the surface of the host material, scrape off the surface itself and take it to the laboratory for analysis. It may contain waxes, cleaners, polish, or detergent that has mixed with the blood and may be important to the chemist to isolate those materials from the blood when performing the analysis.

If the blood has soaked into a porous surface, such as concrete, carpeting, or upholstered furniture, for example, you will have to liquefy the stain in order to collect it. To prepare the stain for collection, use tweezers and dip a small cotton square, or swatch, or a cotton swab into a clean saline solution. Be careful to separate the cotton swatches so as to avoid having two or more stick together. A defense attorney may try to blow up the significance of your counting twenty swatches, then producing more or less during the trial. Little "glitches" like this in your presentation may destroy your credibility in the eyes of a juror or two, no matter how incon-

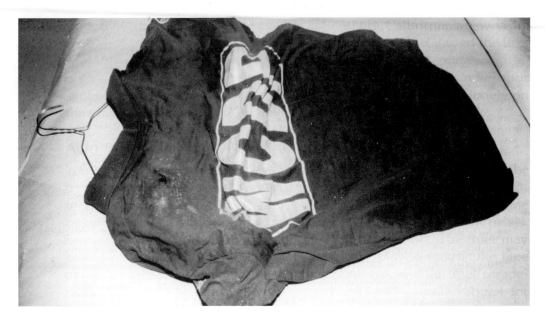

Figure 5.5   To preserve clothing that is saturated with blood, place it on a hanger and wrap it with paper. This will prevent transfer of blood from one area of the clothing to another.

sequential your miscount actually is. Place the wet swatch onto the stain and allow it to soak up as much of the stain as possible. Use as many swatches as necessary until no more of the stain will soak up into a swatch. Place each set of swatches that you use to soak up each of the stains onto separate sheets of clean dry paper, which you will fold loosely into bindles. Give each set of swatches that represent a bloodstain a number that corresponds with the number assigned the stain in your sketch and photographs. To transport these collected samples, place all the bindles into a large paper bag and transport them together to the laboratory. When you later get those individual packets, or bindles containing the blood-soaked swatches, open them up, separate the swatches, and allow them to dry naturally (without using a hair dryer or similar heat source). Be sure to include a sample of the host material for these stains as well because the materials other than the blood have to be separated from the blood for analysis. The laboratory may have a ventilated box with shelves onto which wet samples may be placed to dry, and the box closed and locked for security purposes while drying.

Bloody clothing and bedding, and other similar materials bearing wet blood, should be hung up to dry at the scene before transporting, if

Figure 5.6 If bloody clothes are not properly dried, mold may begin to grow, as in this picture.

possible. If they must be transported while wet, spread them out onto a flat piece of cardboard, then label and transport them without folding or wadding up the material. If you place a wet bloody piece of material in a closed container, mold and putrefaction will begin almost immediately, which will destroy or diminish the evidentiary value of the blood sample. In a sex crime, there might also be semen along with the bloodstains that you will want to preserve as you find it. Folding or packaging such material in a closed container may destroy any spermatozoa that might be present. When you get the wet materials to the laboratory, place them in a secure place and arrange them so that they may air dry.

Blood analysis will tell the analysts that a particular bloodstain conclusively did *not* come from a specified individual or that it probably *did* originate with a specified individual. It will also determine if the stains were from more than one owner. The basic classification system of typing blood as O, A, B, or AB isolates certain percentages of the population, but if the blood of three people shows up in stains at a single crime scene and the persons are types O, A, and B, and the victims have types B and O, that would indicate that the third person—the suspect—had type A blood. But that obviously does not narrow down the field of suspects very much, because millions of people have type A blood. The typing procedure goes far beyond the four basic types, of course, but the real breakthrough in forensic science has been the determination of the genetic code of the person who has that type A blood.

It is possible to determine an individual's DNA, or deoxyribonucleic acid, not only from blood samples but also from many other body
fluids and tissues, including hair if the follicle is attached. The probabilities of narrowing down the list of suspects are phenomenally
greater. Except for identical twins, DNA researchers have estimated that
the chance of any two people in the world having identical DNA is anywhere from 1 in 200,000 to 1 in 5 billion (approximately the current
world population). Once a suspect is located and in custody, a DNA test
can confirm that you probably have the correct suspect. For the past few
years, many laboratories have been maintaining files on the DNA of
people who are being convicted of very serious crimes, including murder, rape, and aggravated assaults. News reports already have informed
us that comparison of those individuals' genetic codes with current and
past unsolved crimes are leading to the solution of crimes that otherwise would be classified as virtually unsolvable.

In addition to blood type and genetic code, analysis of blood and
other body fluids may provide information about alcohol and drug
intake, and some diseases, which may lead the investigation to the suspect's family doctor or rehabilitation center. When collecting blood
samples, take the maximum amount of samples possible. Do not make
the mistake of taking just a few samples with the expectation that what
you have is enough and any more would be a waste of time collecting
and analyzing it. One spot that you miss may be the one spot that identifies a second or third person's injury at the scene. You cannot collect
too much blood.

LIQUIDS OTHER THAN BLOOD

All liquids other than blood believed to have evidentiary value should be
collected, packaged, and transported in the same manner as blood evidence. If it is wet when you find it, keep it wet, if possible. If dry, scrape it
up or soak it up and package it the same as you would blood. Many body
fluids of most people, including urine and feces, will reveal their blood
types and genetic code. A recent case in the Los Angeles area illustrated
this point very clearly. A high school teacher reported that several students had attacked her by throwing feces on her, and she presented the
soiled clothing as proof of the attack. She was eventually convicted of
making a false crime report, because the feces on her clothing was analyzed for DNA and proved to be her own. The prosecutor surmised that
somehow she had soiled herself but was too embarrassed to admit what
had really happened.

FINGERPRINTS

Any place where there are people you are bound to find fingerprints. Residents in a house or employees in an office do not clean their prints off of every object they touch. At a crime scene you will usually find many fingerprints, and sometimes they have been left there by the perpetrator(s). If you find absolutely no prints whatsoever, that in itself is suspicious, because innocent people have no reason to wipe their fingerprints off of objects they touch except to conceal their presence there. We will cover fingerprints in Chapter Eight.

WEAPONS

When one hears the word *weapon*, the first vision that pops into the mind is a gun or a knife. For the purpose of this book, and crime scene investigation in general, a weapon is any instrument or device that is used to attack a person or animal. Besides guns and knives, weapons you will collect include automobiles, motorcycles, bicycles, water hoses, sticks, stones, clubs, baseball bats, golf clubs, books, chairs, kitchen utensils, pencils, and pens, to name a few. Whenever you discover any item that might have been used as a weapon in the crime you are investigating, photograph it in place, draw its location in your sketch, and assign it an appropriate evidence number or letter. Lift the object carefully with a pencil, a hook, or a gripping device while you are wearing gloves to avoid destroying any fingerprints or other traces that might be on the weapon. Place the weapon onto a clean sheet of paper or cardboard, or into a box, and wrap it in such a way that it cannot be inadvertently touched or disturbed while in transit to the evidence locker or laboratory. In your notes, describe the weapon and its overall condition.

Knives

Describe the brand name, if any, the type (hunting, pocket, switchblade, etc.), overall length, blade length, color of the handle, and a general description of the knife, including its apparent condition. Describe any material that may be sticking to the knife.

Guns

Is the gun a semi-automatic pistol or a revolver? Is it a shotgun or a rifle, and what kind of action does it have? What is the overall size of the gun, and what is the barrel length? What is the gauge or caliber? List the name of the manufacturer, the model, and the number. Describe the gun's apparent condition and whether it is loaded or unloaded. Describe the grips or stock. Describe the location of the bullets; whether there are any in the chamber, cylinder, or clip; and whether any had been fired. Describe the location of bullets and shell casings. If bullets are in the cylinder of a revolver, inscribe a number to each receptacle, and list which bullet or shell casing is in which space. All the bullets may be the same, or they may be of more than one brand.

The caliber of a gun is inscribed on the frame, and some are measured in hundredths or thousandths of an inch, such as .22, .25, .32, .38, .45, .357, or .405. The caliber of some guns is measured in millimeters, such as 9mm, which is the same as .38 caliber, or 7.65mm is the same as .32 caliber. Shotguns are measured by gauge, such as 12 or 16. Rifles have a caliber, such as .30, but also may be designated as a 30-06, which means that it was first manufactured in 1906.

If a gun has been fired, look for the bullet holes and the shell casings. A semi-automatic pistol extracts and throws out each shell after it has been fired, whereas the bullets in a revolver are removed with the aid of an ejector after the entire cylinder has been emptied. Extractor marks and ejector marks are different and ballistics will note that difference. Merely finding five or six empty shells on the floor at a shooting scene is not proof that a semi-automatic was fired, as the gun may have been a revolver and the shooter ejected the spent rounds to reload.

Indicate on your sketch the location of all shell casings. Place markers, such as tented numbers next to each one, and photograph them in place. A ballistics expert may be able to determine the location of the shooter by studying the final destination of extracted casings. Loosely defined, ballistics is the study of missiles in flight, and sometimes it is possible to determine the location of a shooter by starting with its final resting place, which may be in the body of a victim, and tracing its flight pattern. For example, a .22 caliber bullet struck a man driving his car along the Interstate 405 freeway through the city of Costa Mesa, California. A ballistics expert was able to pinpoint the probable location from which the bullet was fired. Police officers questioned the resident of the house, and he admitted that he did accidentally fire his .22 rifle while standing in his backyard at the same time as the victim received the wound. Comparison of the rifle and the bullet verified that, in fact, they matched. The house was nearly a mile from the freeway, yet the bullet still had enough strength to penetrate the victim's arm.

When picking up a gun, hold it by its checkered grips or other part where fingerprints and other traces may not be found, while wearing gloves, of course. Unload the gun, following the procedure for cataloging the location of the bullets covered previously. We do not recommend picking up a gun by sticking a pencil into the barrel, because that might alter the rifling or disturb the residue in the barrel. Try moving a handgun by placing a pen in the trigger guard and carry it that way.

Clubs, Sticks, and Other Objects Used as Weapons

Handle all objects that have been or might have been used as weapons with the same care as you would handle guns and knives. Avoid handling any part of the object where you might find fingerprints or other traces, and do not disturb anything that looks as though it may be human blood, tissue or bone fragments, or hair. Include the location of the object in your sketch, photograph it in place before moving it, then pack and transport each item separately before placing it in a larger package that you will use to transport the evidence to the evidence locker or laboratory. Describe the object, including its measurements, and write in your notes the apparent condition of the weapon as you found it.

OTHER EVIDENCE

Tool Marks and Impressions

Chapter Seven is devoted to tool marks, impressions, and the various ways to preserve them. As with weapons and, as a matter of procedure, all items of evidence, draw the objects or give them a representative number and indicate their exact location. Photograph them in place before moving, and be sure to thoroughly describe the objects, their apparent condition, and what relationship they appear to have to the crime under investigation.

Hairs

The expert can determine whether a hair is from an animal or human, its possible racial origin (a person of mixed race may show one heritage more pronounced than another), the age range, possibly the gender, and sometimes the part of the body where the hair had been growing. Certain drugs and narcotics in the owner's body may show up in a hair analysis. In addition to what type of hair spray a person uses, particles found adhering to the cuticle, or outside scaly surface, of the hair may reveal dirt or hay on the farmer, sand on a person who frequents the beach, or dry cement on a concrete worker.

The analyst may be able to make an educated guess as to the owner's gender and approximate age by the hair's length and evidence of grooming, hair coloring, bleach, and conditioner. Closer examination may also show if the hair has been pulled out or if it fell out, was cut or broken, was damaged by a blunt force injury, and whether blood or tissue is present in microscopic amounts. If the hair has been pulled out at the roots, the criminalist may determine the owner's blood type and DNA.

Searching for hairs on clothing, weapons, or the bodies of victims and suspects is a painstaking task, and must be done with strong light, magnifying glasses, tweezers to pick up the hairs, and a great deal of patience. Whether you find a single strand of hair or a handful, indicate in your sketch the location where you find it, photograph in place, and collect and transport the same as you would any other evidence.

When you find hair believed to be evidence at the crime scene, it will be a matter of routine for hair samples to be collected of all suspects and possibly of some of the investigators at the scene for identification and elimination purposes. As a crime scene investigator, it is doubtful that you will be involved in this process during the initial investigation. However, you might be required to collect such samples as a follow-up assignment. When you take samples, collect at least one hundred hairs from at least four quadrants of the head. Draw a chart and indicate which hairs you remove from each quadrant. Pull a few hairs with follicles attached from each section, and cut the rest. If you are going to compare hairs from areas other than the head, cut and pull several hairs from each of those areas of the suspect's body and indicate on your chart the location where each set of hairs are harvested. In sex crimes, the pubic hairs from victim and suspect will be combed to look for foreign hair, as in such a violent contact there is likely to be an exchange of pubic hairs.

Fibers

Fibers may be animal, vegetable, mineral, synthetic, or a combination of two or more of those materials. You may find single fibers on the scene, on the victim, and on the suspect or in his or her vehicle or home. The fibers you find may be attached to buttons or in torn parts of clothing, as if the victim tore them from an attacker's clothing. A nail, a tree or shrub branch, or other sharp object at the scene could have snagged the fibers without the perpetrator being aware that the material had been torn. A violent crime victim might be found in a car trunk or in a location other than where the attack took place, and this can be established by the discovery of carpet fibers on the body and clothing of the victim that are later found to have come from the assailant's living room. You may find a single strand of fiber, or a large piece of material consisting of thousands of strands, and either find may be the one piece of evidence that will make the case and solidify a conviction of the accused.

If many different strands of material are found at a single location, sketch, photograph, and record them as found and then label and package them in the cluster as found. When many strands of fiber are found at different locations, handle each one as a separate item of evidence, numbering or lettering them separately, packaging and transporting them in separate containers to the laboratory. As with other small items of evidence, use tweezers to handle the fibers and, of course, your rubber gloves. Remember to change gloves frequently, particularly when you move from one type of evidence to another to avoid the risk of transferring evidence as well as to avoid criticism for sloppy work. It is better to change gloves too often than too seldom. Keep patches of cloth together so that the criminalist may count the warp and the woof (number of threads in each direction) per square inch.

The expert can identify the manufacturer of the material not only by the weave (warp and woof) of the material but also by the texture and quality. Some colors are used exclusively be certain manufacturers, as are specific styles and designs. The weave of a piece of cloth that you find at the crime scene may match the distinctive color and quality of an article of clothing found on a person suspected of committing the crime. The torn piece and the larger article with the piece missing may actually be matched mechanically by demonstrating the fit as you would fit together two pieces of a jigsaw puzzle. Sometimes in a crime such as a vehicle striking a victim, the impression of the victim's clothing is imprinted onto the painted surface of the vehicle. There are also likely to be small fragments of the material embedded in the paint.

Glass and Glass Fragments

Whenever you have broken glass at the crime scene, you are likely to find particles of the glass spread out over a wide area within "flying distance" of the window, mirror, or other glass object that was broken. The explosive nature of the breaking glass itself plus the force that was used to break the glass will result in glass particles flying onto the skin and clothing of the person breaking the glass and people nearby. It is common for people to get cut by the flying glass as well, particularly if the person breaks the glass with a fist, an elbow, or a foot, for example. Auto safety glass is actually two sheets of glass bound together with a sheet of polyester known as Mylar, and when it breaks it holds together pretty much like a wadded up piece of plastic with all the glass adhering to the plastic. Some types of glass crumble into what appears to be very small pebbles of glass, but most glass breaks into shards and slivers when broken.

When you find a broken panel or sheet of glass, try to keep the larger parts intact as you find them, and collect the many small parts so that the lab technician may attempt to piece the broken parts together like a jigsaw puzzle. They may have come from a single piece of glass or more than one. Also, you are likely to find shards and small particles of glass on the clothing and in the hair of the person who broke the glass and any bystanders there at the time. Sometimes small particles of glass are found in the lab when the criminalist vacuums the suspect's clothing. The criminalist will also be able to match glass particles by their physical content, sometimes the manufacturer, whether the glass came from a car headlamp or window, and many other characteristics of the glass. When you find broken glass and glass particles, locate them in your sketch and notes, photograph them in place, then collect them. Pieces that are found away from the immediate area of the broken source should be packaged and labeled separately, as they may have come from a different source.

It is possible to determine the sequence of bullet holes and whether the bullet came from inside or outside of a pane of glass. When a bullet or similar missile enters the pane of glass, it may shatter the pane completely, or it will make a hole the approximate size of the missile when it enters, then will take more of the glass with it as it comes out the other side, the hole resembling a cone. See Figure 5.7. The fractures that radiate out from the bullet hole are called radial fractures. As these fractures radiate outward from the bullet hole, the energy causes the fracture to continue for varying distances, depending on the velocity of the bullet or other missile. The glass undulates first in the direction of the bullet, then back toward its original location and beyond, in a motion similar to the waves in the ocean. This force on the glass causes fractures that run perpendicular to the radial fractures, giving the glass the appearance of a spider web. See Figure 5.8.

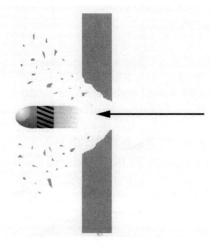

Figure 5.7   This illustration of a bullet going through glass shows that the entrance hole is smaller than the exit. This is helpful when determining direction of travel.

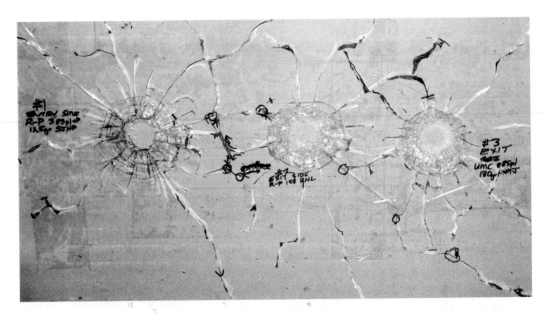

Figure 5.8   By understanding that glass fractures never cross one another, you can determine the sequence in which bullet holes were made.

A second bullet will cause radial and concentric fractures similar to the first shot, but subsequent radial fractures will stop at the place where the earlier one passed. One radial fracture will not cross over an earlier one. Careful examination will show the sequence of the shots fired.

Figure 5.9   In this photograph, there are three glass fractures that stop when they intersect another. This indicates that these fractures were secondary to one another.

Figure 5.10 Wooden dowels are placed through bullet holes to show a bullet's path or trajectory.

If larger pieces are broken out of the frame, it will be possible to photograph the various pieces of glass, make transparencies of the photos, and move them around to try for a mechanical match. A broken pane of glass may have been caused by a blow to the surface, or sometimes a smoldering fire sucking in as much oxygen as it needs will actually cause windows to break inward so as to feed the fire's need for oxygen.

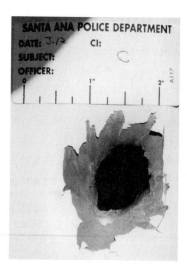

Figure 5.11 By understanding bullet impact, you can determine the approximate angle that this bullet originated from.

Soils, Rocks, and Minerals

Certain regions and neighborhoods have soils, rocks, and minerals that are unique to the area. Raw, undisturbed land that has not been excavated or developed will be easier to locate by its soil characteristics than developed land that has been cleared and stripped of its rock formations, then had a variety of topsoils added from many different parts of the country. In this second type of neighborhood, the developers may have brought in only one or two types of soil, then used a particular type of sod and grass, and treated it with specific brands of fertilizer and pesticide, which may result in such an individual character that some landscape architects may recognize the neighborhood almost immediately by its unique combination of materials.

When soil and rocks are found adhering to the tread of shoes and tires, clothing, or the underside of a vehicle, they may have been picked up at a crime scene and transported by the suspect. These materials may be just the evidence you need to place that person and/or his or her vehicle at the crime scene. Ownership is not enough. You must then prove that the suspect was wearing the shoes or driving the vehicle at the time of the crime. When you find tire or shoe imprints at the scene, take samples of the soil where you find the impressions. From about four different compass points from the impressions that you have photographed and cast, collect three or four tablespoonfuls of the soil and whatever other ingredients it contains. Place each sample in a separate plastic bag that you will seal and label for the laboratory. These samples will be compared with the residue that you remove from the shoe or tire treads of the suspect.

Paint

Every paint manufacturer uses essentially the same ingredients to make its paints, but each has coloring materials and other additives that are copyrighted and unique. Each model of car each year is a different color. The colors are not plain blue or red or yellow, but "robin's egg blue" or "bullfighter flag red" or "sunrise yellow." Even the whites of one car to another are slightly different and may be distinguished by an expert in the laboratory. The same variations occur between manufacturers of paints for all other purposes as well. When you want to match a specific color at the paint store, you bring in a sample and the clerk will mix it for you. When you take a sample to the laboratory, the criminalist will match the exact same color by referring to the color charts of the manufacturers, which they keep on file and continuously update as new colors are created.

When you pick up chips of paint at the scene, or scrape a sample off of a surface that has been struck by a car, such as another car or a building, indicate on your sketch exactly where you found it and photograph it in place. Then package and transport it as any other item of evidence. Several scrapings from a single location may be placed in the same bag or paper bindle, but samples found at different locations should be bagged separately. When you take paint scrapings from a vehicle that also has paint transfers from another vehicle, scrape the sample at the location where the transfer took place, as the damage has already been done. In other cases, choose a part of the car where the removal of the paint is not going to destroy the outward appearance of the car, such as on the underside of a door or interior of a trunk. Scrape all the way down to the bare metal, which will probably reveal several layers of paint and primer in the same sequence as when the car was painted at different times. Going down to the original color on a piece of the car left at the scene of a hit and run, for example, will lead to identification of the make and model of the suspect vehicle.

Liquids

Collect liquids with a bulb and syringe or a turkey baster and try to keep them in their liquid state by sealing the container. Alcoholic beverages must be sealed in a glass or metal container so that the alcohol will not evaporate. In order to avoid diluting the beverage further, be sure to remove any ice cubes that might be in the drink. Refrigerate but do not freeze the liquid evidence.

The components of flammable liquids, such as those that have been used to start arson fires, can be identified in the laboratory. Sometimes it is possible not only to say that the liquid is gasoline, but that it is 87 octane Shell gasoline (or other brand). Sometimes the incendiary material found at the fire scene can be compared with the contents of a can of gasoline found at the suspect's home, and the expert may state with assurance that the gasoline used to start the fire probably came from the can at the home of the suspect.

Other liquids can be identified and may prove to be valuable evidence in your case. A glass of soda might be used to show a suspect's taste for a particular brand of soda. A beverage containing medication may give the criminalist a clue as to a medical problem that the owner of the beverage may have, and indirectly lead to a suspect through his or her medical records.

Wood

Wood may be identified by species, such as oak, elm, ash, and so forth. A piece of wood found at the scene of a crime may be a broken piece of a certain type of tool, such as a hammer or axe handle. Two broken pieces of wood may be matched mechanically (jigsaw method) or by species, or by how they are treated with stain or varnish. Wood chips or sawdust tracked into the crime scene may indicate that the perpetrator came from a construction site, or was perhaps working in a shop at home. Also, the scene of the crime may have sawdust from recent construction work, and the perpetrator may have taken some away from the scene on his or her clothing, or between shoe or tire treads. Photograph, catalogue, and handle as other pieces of dry evidence in case the wood or sawdust might later prove to be relevant to the case.

Documents

Crimes involving documentary evidence usually originate in the home or office. They involve forgery, fraud, embezzlement, theft by trick and device, false representation, and many others. What you are looking for, of course, depends on the crime, but writing, typing, and printing instruments may yield clues to help solve the crime. Documents have to be written or printed. Pens, pencils, typewriters, computers, notebooks, and paper are all items worth close scrutiny.

Sophisticated crime schemes may be found on computer programs, with forms, letters, and other information in the program. A computer expert can sometimes have success in cracking the code and getting by gates with formulas for figuring out passwords. Typewriter ribbons and the surface of the roller, or platen, may be impressed with the text from a recently typewritten document that may be of evidentiary value. Pens and pencils contain ink and graphite that may be so unique that particular items can be identified as the instruments that were used to produce certain incriminating documents.

Forged and fraudulent checks, loan documents and securities, extortion notes, and threatening letters all originated with some person, and with the aid of certain instruments. The objective is to connect the documents with the instruments and their makers. Sometimes the suspect has shredded, torn up, or burned documents that are needed for evidence. Collect the shredder and the wastebasket containing the shredded material. It may be possible to reconstruct some of the shredded document, if not all. Burned documents may hold together in their charred state until you touch them, then crumble into ashes. Photograph them as you find any of these items before you attempt to handle them in any way. If you place a solid piece of cardboard underneath the charred document and lightly spray with a fixative, such as hair spray, you may be able to hold it together. If you are successful so far, make sure you have photographs of the document in its present state just in case it falls apart as you proceed. Place the

Figure 5.12   In this illustration, whiteout has been used to cover up some writing.

document in a box so that it will not be disturbed further until it gets to the lab. The lab technician will probably attempt to place the charred document between two pieces of glass for further analysis.

Checks, checkbooks, and documents that appear to belong to someone other than the occupant of the business or house may be forgeries. If the owner or occupant of the premises is present, ask for a statement of ownership, and record the responses that person gives you. Include in your report the data about where you found the documents and other materials, and handle them the same as any other evidence.

When the victim claims that his or her name, logo, and other personal identifying data, such as checks or credit cards or letterheads, have been forged for the unlawful use of another person, have that person sign an affidavit of forgery. This will probably best be done later by a follow-up investigator or in the prosecuting attorney's office. You will also need exemplars of the victim's and the suspect's writing, typing, printing, and so forth, as applicable to the particular case under investigation, which you should secure as quickly as possible.

Preparation of the Exemplar

Depending on the crime, you will want to get a sample of the suspect's writing. Your department may have a standard form that it uses, but we suggest that you make your own form, customized to the specific crime. For example, in a highly publicized Colorado murder case, which is still

Figure 5.13 By using a strong back light, the ink underneath the whiteout can be read.

under investigation at the time of writing this chapter and which will continue for years, the victim's family found a ransom note and turned it over to the investigators. The one thing you should not do is to hand a suspect a copy of the note and have him or her copy it. Not only are the handwriting experts looking to compare the handwriting, but they are also looking for grammatical structure, spelling, punctuation, and overall composition. By letting the suspect look at the original while trying *not* to copy it, you would be destroying the value of having that person prepare an exemplar at all. Dictate the words you want the person to write, but do not spell the words or dictate the punctuation as though you were dictating a business letter. If you had a dyslexic suspect and a ransom note with numerous misspelled words, you certainly would not want to spell words that you dictate to the suspect.

Miscellaneous Trace Evidence

During your crime scene investigation you will come across something that we have not covered in this text, but your police officer senses tell you that it might have some evidentiary value. Whenever you do come across such an item, photograph it in place, record it in your report, and process it as evidence. As the investigation proceeds, many of the items that you collect may prove to be of value to the case, and many others will lead to dead ends. It is better to collect too much evidence than too little. In the final analysis, you may have done a better job collecting more evidence than you need than if you missed a crucial item that is lost forever once you have left the crime scene.

PACKAGING AND LABELING EVIDENCE

In this chapter we have discussed some of the methods for collecting and preserving evidence. In addition to those instructions we have already covered, here are some basic guidelines: If the item is large enough and there is space on the object where you can inscribe your logo or other identifying data without destroying the monetary or evidentiary value, do so directly on the object. Smaller items cannot be marked directly and you must place them in suitable containers. In all cases attach an evidence label to the object itself or to the container, listing the number or letter designation of the item, date, time, case number, your logo or initial, and to whom or in what locker you placed the item. Containers are glass vials, paper bags, self-sealing plastic bags, new paint cans for flammable liquids, boxes made of wood or cardboard with string to hold items in place, and packing Styrofoam "popcorn" to keep items from moving about while in transit. Place your logo on the container and attach the evidence tag.

Figure 5.14 Proper care must be taken when handling and packaging evidence depending on its relevance to the scene.

CHAIN OF CUSTODY

We have covered the chain of custody procedure earlier in the text, but just a word to remind you that from the moment the evidence is collected until the moment it is introduced in court as evidence, there must be an unbroken chain of custody of every item of evidence. This is extremely crucial to every case.

SUMMARY

As you can see, evidence comes in many shapes and guises, sometimes presenting itself to you when you do not even recognize it as evidence. Consider the type of crime you are investigating and seek out those items of evidence to prove each element of the *corpus delicti*, then look for whatever else you can find that might be even remotely related to the case. Sometimes one crime is committed to cover another, such as arson to conceal a murder, or a so-called "victim" may fabricate a crime story and create a crime scene to back it up. Your investigation is to determine what crime, if any, took place, and to collect as much evidence as possible to establish the facts. Remember that you can never collect too much evidence.

SUGGESTED OUTSIDE PROJECTS

1. Create your own file of tire designs. Go to the various dealers and ask for brochures with photographs of tire treads, and take photographs of as many different tread designs as you can find. Continue this project for six to eight weeks. (After you complete the course, continue updating this file as each new design comes out.)

2. From your imaginary crime scene, collect and package the following items that represent evidence: an alcoholic beverage containing ice cubes, paint scrapings from the interior of a car's trunk, a knife, a gun, a screwdriver or hammer, a torn piece of clothing, several strands of hair, and a wet article of clothing. Photograph them as you have them packaged, and attach evidence tags on each.

DISCUSSION QUESTIONS

1. Describe the process of chain of custody and why it is important to a crime investigation.

2. When you find a dried bloodstain, how do you remove it from the surface?

3. What do the letters DNA stand for?

4. What is a *stride pattern* and what can it tell the experienced investigator?

5. From what body products may the laboratory determine a person's DNA?

6. Can blood type be used to identify a suspect positively? Why? Why not?

7. When you find trace evidence at the scene, what is the principal reason for you to photograph it before attempting to collect it?

8. How do you keep blood in its liquid state in a glass bottle or jar?

9. Explain the *radial* and *concentric* fractures in glass.

10. How can you tell that one bullet hole in a window was made before another one?

Chapter Six
Evidence by Type of Crime

INTRODUCTION

In the preceding chapter we covered evidence by type and category and methods of collecting the evidence. In this chapter we approach the subject from the aspect of what one might find in different types of crimes. In addition to what one must regard as evidence, there are other discoveries you might make during your investigation that may not be admissible in court but still help isolate and identify the perpetrators. For example, as we noted earlier in the text, food missing from a refrigerator may indicate that a burglar has a taste for cottage cheese and leftovers, but that fact, in itself, does not prove guilt. What it does tell you, however, is that eating on the job may be part of the perpetrator's modus operandi and is a behavior pattern that shows up in every crime that he or she commits. You might even start calling this culprit "the hungry burglar." In this chapter we will make a few suggestions to aid in your investigation.

CRIMES AGAINST PERSONS

Criminal Homicide

The most obvious item you should hope to find is the weapon or other means with which the perpetrator committed the act. When you first observe the body of the deceased, you may look at the fatal wound and hastily decide what type of weapon caused the wounds. Be careful! All wounds are not what they appear to be. For example, what appears to be a small-caliber bullet hole may have actually been made with a stiletto or an ice pick, or perhaps even a screwdriver; whereas a blunt force wound may tear the skin in such a way so as to appear as though it were made with a knife. Assume nothing while searching for weapons, and collect all objects that even remotely suggest that they have any relationship to the crime. The moral of this advice is that you should not limit your imagination or you will miss crucial evidence.

Relatives or friends of the victims commit many homicides. Although proof of a motive is not necessary to prove the elements of a crime, it will certainly help focus the investigation if the reason for the crime were known. Some of the questions an investigator should ask him or her are: Who would benefit most by this death? Or who wanted to see this person dead? Was there a great amount of money, a long-standing hatred, or a desire for revenge that motivated this murder? Is there a new love in the suspected killer's life with a third party in the way of this blossoming love? Is there a sizable insurance policy, and who is the beneficiary?

Look for threatening letters or diary entries that might indicate a problem relationship, such as broken marriages or relationships, philandering spouses, or jealous lovers. Telephone and address books might provide names and other information about friends, relatives, or business associates. Telephone bills that list long-distance phone calls may lead to discovery of people the victim may have called regarding his or her fears of impending doom. Personal papers and correspondence will provide names and addresses of others who may have some information about the victim's life, which may have caused concern for the victim's safety. Some individuals get violent and retaliate when served with a restraining order. Perhaps the victim had testified against someone in a criminal trial that led to a conviction, and the murder is in retaliation for the testimony.

Are there signs of violence on the premises, such as broken lamps, overturned furniture, or other disturbed furniture? Does everything in the place look *too* neat, as though it had been cleaned up, including removal of latent prints from all objects that the perpetrator might have touched? What is missing from the scene that should be there, such as jewelry, clothing, or other personal items belonging to the victim? Some perpetrators make a habit of collecting souvenirs to remind them of their crimes for their morbid sense of sentimentality. Cannibals like Jeffrey Dahmer collect body parts and keep them in the refrigerator and other places around their houses because it creates some sort of a bond between perpetrator and victim long after death.

Was there a forced entry and/or exit indicating that the perpetrator did not have a key? Or was entry made by invitation of the victim, or by someone who had a key to the premises? Someone who ever borrowed or had temporary possession of a key and returned it could still have made a copy quite easily. Did the victim appear to have known the perpetrator, indicated by such things as two or three cocktail glasses or beer bottles, or more than one serving for a meal served at the approximate time of the murder? Did the killer(s) leave anything behind at the scene, such as an article of clothing or other personal item that had not been at the scene before the crime? A spouse or a frequent visitor may provide you with this kind of information.

If the victim shows signs of life, the first officer(s) on the scene may have had to damage or destroy evidence in order to administer first aid, but that is just something you have to take in stride. If the victim is still at the scene and you have already determined that death has, in fact, occurred, take photographs of the victim in the position he or she was found. Only the coroner, a medical examiner, a paramedic, or other qualified individual may pronounce death. You may see that the victim is dead by the absence of pulse and respiration (which are presumptive signs of death, but not positive), as well as livor mortis (postmortem lividity), rigor mortis, decomposition, and other positive signs of death. After you have completed photographing and sketching the body in place as it was found, the coroner will then take custody of the body. The body is the jurisdictional responsibility of the coroner, but the crime investigation is the responsibility of your department. The coroner's people will not remove the body from the scene until you and your colleagues have finished the part of the investigation that requires that you keep the body in place.

Sometimes the perpetrator makes a homicide appear as though a death were a suicide or an accident. For that reason, you should approach every dead body case as though it were a criminal homicide until the investigation determines that the death was not caused by the "criminal act of another," as the coroner would classify such a death. There are times when even an accidental death turns out to have been the result of someone's criminal negligence, at which time it becomes a criminal case again. A phony doctor who performs an illegal surgery, for example, is committing murder if the patient dies.

Assault

In many cases, felony and misdemeanor assaults are distinguished by the weapon used to commit the crime. Use of a gun or a knife in assaults classifies them as felonies; whereas assaults with such weapons as baseball bats, automobiles, and other objects may be either felonies or misdemeanors, depending on the nature of the injuries the victim sustains. Some assaults may be listed as felonies or misdemeanors depending on the investigating officers' initial evaluation of the injuries sustained by the victim They may be reclassified later as the more or less serious crime depending on what the doctors say after they have taken X-rays and conducted a preliminary examination of the victim.

Sometimes it is not possible to determine the exact nature and extent of the crime during the initial phase of the investigation. Many victims and witnesses are shocked and confused, or uncooperative. Maybe they are not sure about what happened, or perhaps a loved one inflicted the wounds and you have a reluctant witness. Another problem you will have determining the extent of a victim's injuries is that some people have a high or low threshold of pain, whereas others have a tendency to exaggerate or minimize their pain.

Until you know what weapon was used to inflict an injury, look for any weapon or device that the perpetrator might have used. Some articles may have blood, hairs, or tissue attached and should certainly be considered suspect. Photograph the suspected weapon and collect it as described in Chapter Five.

Robbery

Although it is classified as a crime against property because the objective is to get property from another by means of force or fear, we classify it here as a personal crime because the robbery is most often accomplished with some type of assault or threatened assault. At the "nutrition bar" where all the snack machines are located near the school cafeteria, the bully who forcibly takes money from another child is committing a robbery. Although he or she does not use a weapon, we call that a "strong-arm robbery." Regardless of whether the bully actually assaults the victim beyond the forceful grabbing and holding, or how much money is taken from the victim, it is still a robbery. A carjacking, which involves taking a vehicle from its driver by force and/or fear, is also a robbery.

Look for the weapon that was used or that the suspect threatened to use at or near the scene. Some robbers discard the weapon so as to be unarmed if stopped by officers for questioning, whereas others retain it as a souvenir to remember the moment and to use again. Have the victims and witnesses repeat verbatim, if possible, the words used by the suspect while committing the crime. Sometimes a witness may recognize a foreign or regional accent, and some robbers use exactly the same words when committing their robberies, perhaps because they think it brings them luck, or because it works so well in getting results. Some robbers ask for a specific object or amount of money, which is that robber's trademark, and some even apologize and try to explain why they are committing the crime. We have a tendency to give some robbers nicknames based on their behavior, such as "the gentleman robber," "the robber with the sick baby," or "the lunch bucket bandit" because he carries a child's lunch box to carry his loot. These monickers help investigators tie a string of robberies together by modus operandi and facilitate the robbers' arrest because it is sometimes possible to anticipate a robbery. Then they place a surveillance on a prospective place of business, or dress up an officer as a decoy to trap the perpetrators (we said "trap," not "entrap," you will note).

Child Abuse

Pay close attention to the child's room. An abused child sometimes takes out his or her anger on toys or personal objects because the person who abused them—perhaps a parent or older sibling—is so much bigger, stronger, and authoritative. The child may keep a journal or diary documenting the occasions of abuse. Corporal punishment is not, in itself, against the law. In many cultures it is normal for parents or elders to spank or slap children to discipline them. What is against the law is when the punishment goes "over the line," whatever that boundary is in the eyes of the investigator and eventually the courts and the juries.

Question the child and the parents and other persons involved separately. Never question a child whom you think may have been abused in

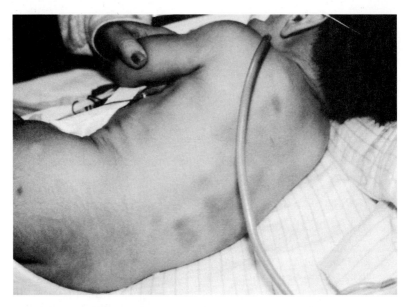

Figure 6.1 When photographing bruises, note the different colors or stages of healing that the bruises are in. This can be an indicator of repeated and ongoing abuse.

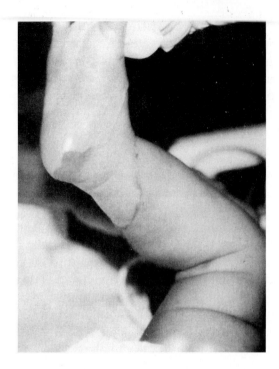

Figure 6.2 The different degrees of blistering and peeling skin can indicate the degrees of burns as in the case of child abuse.

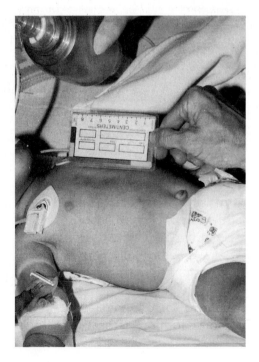

Figure 6.3 Often internal injuries cannot be documented. In such a case, photograph any external injuries that may collaborate with internal injuries.

the presence of his or her parent, thus avoiding any hint of undue pressure on the child to change the story about how certain injuries were inflicted. As the crime scene investigator you may not be the person to handle the questioning. But in case you are, it may be better just to get the bare essentials about the nature of the injuries, and leave the in-depth interview about how the injuries happened for the juvenile experts to handle. Your responsibility is to take photographs of the places where the injuries took place, make an accurate sketch, and report all of the evidence that you find that either substantiates or disproves a parent's story about how the injuries occurred. For example, a doctor can usually tell whether a child fell and broke an arm, or whether someone broke it by twisting it, or whether a child fell down the stairs or was thrown down by an angry adult.

Kidnap

Sometimes what is alleged to have been a kidnapping may not be a kidnap at all. Regardless of what the parents or other reporting parties tell you or your colleagues, the first place you search are the premises from where the child was reportedly taken. Look in places where you might expect to find a child alive but also look in places where you might find a dead child or where someone may have hidden the child's dismembered body parts. Do not overlook the refrigerator and freezer, or trash dumpster out back or down the street. The kidnap may actually have been a physical or sexual abuse gone horribly wrong, and the kidnap story is manufactured to divert the investigation somewhere other than the direction it should go.

If a ransom note was found, collect all the types of devices that the author might have used on the premises, including pens, pencils, typewriters, computers. If the note was made up of words clipped out of magazines and newspapers, collect any of those items from which the clippings may have been taken. Even if you have no reason to suspect the family members of the crime, it is still possible that the kidnappers prepared the note while in the house. Your investigation may lead to a family member as the actual culprit, and what would have been done to the evidence had you not collected all these materials when you were on the premises? To take them for "elimination" purposes during your initial search would not have required a search warrant. If the note is handwritten, you will also want to get handwriting exemplars from all family members for "elimination" purposes. Do not have anyone look at, or copy, the ransom note to prepare the exemplar.

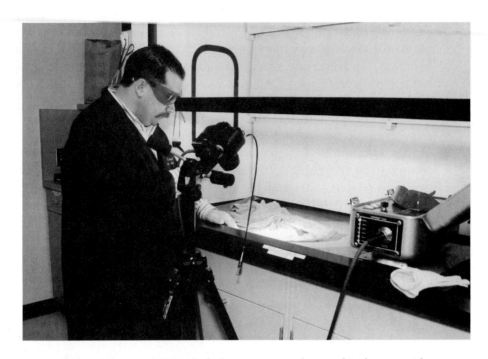

Figure 6.4   An alternate light source can be used to locate and document biological fluids such as semen, which will fluoresce. Photographs can then be taken showing the location of the evidence.

Sex Crimes

Forcible rape or a violent child molestation come to mind when one first hears the term *sex crimes,* although many sex crimes are committed fraud, or trickery, or the victim may be unconscious while the crime is being committed. The victim may not know that what is happening is even a crime. What a child may think of as normal play with an older friend or member of the family (or even a stranger) may be a sexual molestation. But the child feels no pain and has no information that such behavior is legally and morally wrong. Therefore, unless someone else observes the behavior, or if it is revealed during a conversation with the child, it will probably go undetected, perhaps beyond the statute of limitations. Then the child grows up and learns years later that what Uncle Charlie used to do with him or her was actually a molestation.

For a variety of reasons, some rape victims fail or decline to report the crime, perhaps because they erroneously feel guilty for letting themselves get into such a situation. A person in a position of power over the victim, such as an employer, may make sexual advances and the victim

Figure 6.5   Here the evidence is seen with the light source illuminating it without any color filtration.

will not file a criminal complaint for fear of losing her job or not getting a promotion. Or perhaps the boss promises her an increase in salary in exchange for her silence, and she may be in dire need of more money to make ends meet. Many reported rape cases are approached by defense attorneys as though the victim were actually the aggressor, and the attacker an innocent victim. "What does this have to do with crime scene investigation?" you ask. The items of evidence you need are such seemingly innocent alcoholic beverages and hypnotic drugs, such as the "date rape" drugs. The suspect may have convinced the victim that they should go

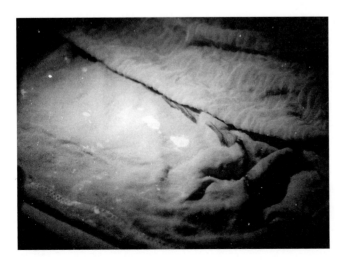

Figure 6.6   This is the same evidence viewed under orange filtration with the stains now made visible.

someplace in his vehicle, leaving her car behind, thereby placing her in a situation where the pressure is to "put out or walk home."

A doctor or nurse will be the only person to examine the victim and collect evidence from her body and to examine the body of the suspect for similar evidence, such as exchanged public hairs and body fluids, saliva, physical evidence of sexual penetration, and other related materials. Your task as crime scene investigator is to look for similar substances at the scene of the alleged sex act to determine if there was any evidence of sexual contact.

A very serious problem in a rape case is the traumatic condition of the victim, who may compulsively start cleaning the room, taking a douche and bath, and putting the bedclothes into the washing machine, all to clean away the "filth." Search for items that may have been placed in a clothes hamper or washing machine that may yield evidence of the sex act. Look for signs that a struggle may have taken place, lending credence that the act was entirely involuntary. Some rape suspects, particularly in those cases sometimes referred to as date rapes, may resort to their defense that "all women fight at first before they give in."

In the child molestation case, you are looking for evidence of a sex act having taken place somewhere at or near where the child described it had occurred. If the crime took place in the suspect's place of residence, search for any photographs, movies, videotapes, or any other material that might tend to prove the suspect's preference for children rather than women his own age. You may find children's toys or clothing and other things that you might find in a child's room, such as special wallpaper or bedding. The pedophile may consider himself a child in spirit, thereby "explaining" his pedophilia.

Some rapes are committed by fraud, such as phony marriages, where there is consensual sex, but the consent is based on the belief that the marriage was lawful. Both prosecution and defense may stipulate that there was consensual sex, especially if the couple had sex on more than one occasion. That type of rape is more of a document-related crime, yet still a sex crime, but the sex act is overshadowed by the fraudulent act of the perpetrator. A doctor or dentist may sexually assault or rape a victim who is under sedation and unable to resist or who might be totally unconscious at the time of the act. In addition to collecting whatever evidence is available to establish that a sex act took place, the utilization of hidden video cameras and women working undercover as decoys may lead to the suspect actually attempting to commit the rape while under surveillance or investigation . This would aid in establishing a pattern of behavior, which would tend to prove that there were unlawful sex acts being committed upon unsuspecting women in the sanctity of the examining room.

In some rape or molestation cases, the perpetrator may have used sex "toys" and other paraphernalia in addition to, or instead of, his actual body parts. In that case you have an additional crime, rape with a foreign object, or sexual battery in addition to or instead of rape. In a case of that nature, you must present the object that was used to commit the act.

CRIMES AGAINST PROPERTY

Arson

One very important note regarding photographing fire scenes is that you must remember to open up the aperture a couple of F-stops to allow more light into the camera, and your lighting is going to have to be brighter and at a different angle. Charred wood and other charred surfaces have a tendency to suck up light like a sponge sucks up water. Before you take photos at a fire scene, take a few practice shots to get used to the idea that you are not washing out the picture so that you will have the freedom to "open up" for the fire scenes.

Figure 6.7 When a person is burned, the muscles contract causing the arms and legs to bend as seen in this photograph. Courtesy of Sheriff's Department, San Diego, California.

Figure 6.8 Lightbulbs are good indicators at an arson scene because they tend to swell in the direction of the most intense heat, which may be a clue as to the point of origin in a fire. Courtesy of Sheriff's Department, San Diego, California.

Although much of the evidence in arson cases is destroyed by fire, well-trained fire investigators are experts in locating the point of origin, or the place where the fire started, as well as the incendiary device or material and accelerants used to start the fire and to keep it going. Charred wood may be saturated with kerosene or gasoline, a pile of oily rags might still be smoldering, and candle wax or remnants of a fuse may indicate how the fire was ignited. There may be some sort of device that sparks when set off, such as a telephone, an electric switch, or a doorbell that was placed among some highly flammable material that started the fire. If the arsonist is the owner or a tenant of the property, you might not get the cooperation you need, but he or she may still provide valuable information by describing the condition of the place when last seen, which may be verified or refuted by other witnesses, or proven to be false by evidence you find at the scene.

A tenant or owner who starts a fire himself or herself or who hires a "torch" to do the job may replace expensive furniture and other personal treasures from the premises with junk from a thrift shop before the fire. A witness who is familiar with the premises might be able to spot this difference, whereas you would have no idea that such a switch took place. In

Figure 6.9 Burn patterns can show the point of origin at a fire or area of most intense heat. Courtesy of Sheriff's Department, San Diego, California.

a cocktail lounge fire in Newport Beach a few years ago, the firefighters discovered that most of the liquor bottles in the storeroom were broken, ostensibly by the fire or the people attempting to put it out before the fire department arrived. Closer examination led the investigators to discover that the broken bottles had been full of something other than liquor when broken. The investigators discovered that the lounge owners had another place in Santa Ana, and they were able to secure a search warrant for that place. In the storeroom of the bar in Santa Ana, they found dozens of cases of liquor that had been delivered to the lounge in Newport Beach. Liquor dealers code the cases of liquor for specific destinations, the investigators discovered. The owners of the two places were convicted for bankruptcy and insurance fraud as well as soliciting for an arson.

Another hint for the photographer is to take photos of the bystanders who are watching the firefighters and investigators at work. Perpetrators have been known to return to the scene to check on their handiwork, sometimes even pitching in and helping wherever they can. A recent Southern California series of fires was found to have been started by a highly respected arson investigator, who was convicted for arson and murder, because people died in one of the fires he started. Some fires were started in the city of San Marino, also in Southern California, a few years ago and the investigation led to a police patrol officer who started the fires so that he could start putting them out and call the fire department. The police chief and other civic leaders had lauded the officer as a hero for saving lives by finding the fires. It turned out that he was just lonely on the graveyard watch and hungry for attention.

Auto Theft

You may be able to identify the perpetrator by carefully searching the recovered vehicle that had been stolen. Check the mirror and seat adjustment for a clue as to the thief's size, whether it is approximately the same as, or different from that of the car's owner. Always look for latent prints. Some thieves do not wear gloves or wipe off their prints. The thief may have a certain taste in radio stations or may have played a particular tape or compact disc that he or she liked, which may be part of the thief's trademark. Check the ashtray, glove compartment, and console cabinet for items removed or left behind (theory of transference). Has the thief left behind any tools or articles of clothing, or perhaps picked up a passenger who left one of those objects behind without the knowledge of the thief?

Some car owners pay professional car thieves to steal their cars so that they might collect the insurance, but you probably would not be able to find that out by investigating the crime scene. It may seem unusual, however, if the victim left the keys in the car so that the thief did not have to hot-wire it.

Burglary

Sometimes it is possible to determine whether the intruder was familiar with the premises, or he or she knew where to look for the object taken in the burglary. Besides the dresser or cabinet drawer from where valuables were removed, was anything else disturbed? Did the intruder stumble or fall over any of the furniture, or knock over a lamp while groping around in the dark? Have books on the bookshelves been moved or removed, or other possible hiding places for money been moved or destroyed?

Which lights were turned on or off during the intrusion and which ones were left on? What was the method of entry? Was a tool used, or had the owner left the door or a window unlocked upon leaving the premises earlier? A friend of one of the authors recently lost a nanny, who said she was going back home to her mother country. The lady of the house went into the bedroom, took her cash box out of its hiding place, and removed the nanny's pay for the week. This friend teaches private acting classes and stores a lot of her cash in the box (possibly to avoid notifying the tax people of her considerable cash income). She bade the nanny goodbye and left the nanny in charge of her child for the last day, and when she returned home a few hours later, the nanny and the cash box were gone. Fortunately the nanny had left behind her young daughter. It was easy for the investigators to figure out who stole the box full of several thousand dollars in cash.

Outside the premises there may be signs that the burglar lingered for a while, may have left shoe prints, discarded candy or chewing gum wrappers, or perhaps smoked a cigarette or two while waiting for his victim to leave so that he could enter during the victim's absence. Look for signs that a vehicle may have been parked nearby. Also search trash cans and dumpsters to see if the burglar discarded any of the loot, such as purses or wallets.

Theft

Many thefts are "crimes of opportunity," which involve no witnesses and no evidence. Nevertheless, work on the theory of transfer, and search for any item the perpetrator may have taken away from the scene and lost or discarded along the way. When a thief steals a purse or wallet, he or she will usually take out only the cash and a credit card and discard the rest, so that there will not be any incriminating evidence on his or her person in the event of being stopped and questioned by the police. You may be in luck and find something that belongs to the thief that he or she inadvertently left behind, or some item the thief decided to keep for sentimental reasons.

Pawnshops, secondhand stores, garage sales, and swap meets are some of the places follow-up investigators will look for stolen merchandise, but there is little that the crime scene investigator can do in this type of crime. Some departments take reports over the telephone or have victims come into the office to make their reports because of the futility of looking for evidence. A quick search of the vehicle for possible latent prints may yield a smudge or two, but is not likely.

SUMMARY

Perhaps several of the suggestions in this chapter may aid in your crime scene search. Do not be discouraged when you conduct an exhaustive search and do not find all the evidence you are looking for. In some cases you may not find any evidence at all. What is important is that your search must be as thorough as possible and not be sloppy or unprofessional. Home run champions strike out half of the time at bat, and you are going to strike out sometimes. The point in this chapter is to keep looking until you find little or nothing. Never approach a crime scene with a defeatist attitude that there is no use searching because you are not going to find anything. Always operate on the theory that the perpetrator leaves something at the scene and takes something away from the scene. Many times it may only be a memory or a shadow, but perhaps forensic science will be developed to the point someday that even memories and shadows may be turned into tangible evidence.

SUGGESTED OUTSIDE PROJECTS

1. Put together a sample ransom note without use of a pen, a computer, or a typewriter. Make all the words and sentences out of clippings from newspapers, magazines, and other printed sources.

2. Do some research and describe at least seven different types of devices that an arsonist might use to start a fire from a remote location. Draw sketches or diagrams of each, and describe how it would work. You may choose to seek the assistance of someone from your local arson investigation squad.

DISCUSSION QUESTIONS

1. Why is it necessary to collect all items that may have been used as a weapon in a homicide even though you have a pretty solid idea that the weapon used was the gun found next to the body?

2. According to your local police and sheriff's department, what percentage of homicides are committed by friends or members of the family?

3. If you are the first person to arrive at the scene of a homicide, what is the *first* thing you must do?

4. What are *presumptive* signs of death? Give two examples.

5. What are *positive* signs of death? Give five examples.

6. In your jurisdiction, can a person commit a robbery without using a weapon?

7. Is it possible for a child to be sexually abused without knowing it? If so, give an example.

8. Can a married woman be raped in your jurisdiction?

9. What is the difference between taking photographs at an arson scene and taking photos at a burglary scene?

10. Why are so many petty thefts not solved?

Chapter Seven
Impression Evidence

INTRODUCTION

We operate on the theory of transference; that is, we expect the perpetrator to leave something behind at the crime scene and take something away from it. It is a simple fact that a person can hardly move about the crime scene without leaving behind imprints of his or her shoes, feet, wheels (if using a wheelchair), or pogo stick. Then, when the victims arrive home and the police arrive to investigate the crime, their own movements about the scene tend to obliterate those left by the perpetrators. For that reason, shoe prints are often referred to as the "missed evidence." With this evidentiary problem in mind, in the perfect world the victims would back off and call the police without entering the premises, and the officers upon arrival would search the floor and ground surfaces for impressions before entering. In this chapter, we discuss what may be done with impression evidence when you are fortunate enough to find some at the crime scene.

Evidentiary Value of Impression Evidence

Shoe prints, tire prints, and other impressions can be matched "beyond all reasonable doubt" by their characteristics. (Remember, only death and taxes are absolute.) Impressions found at a crime scene can be compared with shoes, socks, tires, tools, and other objects that made those impressions to such an extent that the criminalist or lab technician can declare a match with virtual certainty. As people go about their daily business of walking, driving, or using tools in their work or hobbies, all these devices wear down in unique ways. Sharp rocks, glass, or other hard foreign objects will make their distinctive marks on the softer surfaces, which will be unlike marks made on any other similar object such as a shoe or tire.

Normal and abnormal wear and tear on these objects will also be unique. When the actual object is compared to an impression suspected of having been made by that object, all of these wear patterns and cuts and gouges will create a mirror image of their characteristics on the materials with which they come in contact.

When there are a sufficient number of these identifying characteristics brought out during the comparison process, the expert will then testify as to the match. The next step is to put the perpetrator in those shoes, socks, or vehicle, or in possession of those impression-making objects. Even when there are not sufficient unique characteristics and a positive match is not possible, the impression will reveal different class comparisons, such as approximate size and/or weight of a suspect by shoe size. It is possible to determine the manufacturer by shoe or tire patterns. The pattern of impressions may reveal the length and width of a vehicle, or the approximate height of a suspect by the stride pattern, the length of the steps taken by the suspect. Deeper impressions at the heels may indicate that the person was carrying a heavy weight, and deeper impressions of the sole portion of the shoe may indicate that the suspect was running. With these bits of information, investigators may be able to narrow down their lists of possible suspects at least.

The Search

Give careful consideration to all contingencies while conducting your search for impressions of any kind. Some impressions may be more easily recognized whereas others are more difficult because of the surface onto which the impressions have been made. As with your search for fingerprints and other traces, aim a flashlight across the surface at an oblique angle, which will more readily reveal any impressions that are present. Once you locate an impression, be careful to protect it until you can properly document and collect it. Cover the impression to protect it from the weather, and mark it off with tape, traffic cones, or numbered tents to keep people from stepping on or otherwise destroying the impression. Take photographs before attempting to remove or make impressions of any evidence.

Photographing the Impression

In order to obtain maximum contrast of impressions, take all of your photographs with black-and-white film. Begin by placing your camera on a tripod directly over the impression, making sure that the film plane is precisely parallel with the surface. This is crucial to avoid distortion of the image when the photograph is produced in the darkroom. Check with

Figure 7.1 Use an L-shaped ruler to measure the shoe prints' width and length. Also include an information card with a NORTH arrow, case number, evidence number, date, time, and your name.

Figure 7.2 Take an overall photograph of where the shoe print evidence is located to aid in orientation and direction of travel.

your photographic expert to make sure that you are using the correct camera lens for your camera. Place an L-shaped ruler next to the impression so that it measures both the length and width of the impression. Place an identifier card alongside the impression with a NORTH arrow to show direction as well as the case number, evidence item number, date and time of the crime, and date and time you take the photograph.

The first photo should be an overall orientation shot using the flash at a normal "straight-on" angle. Because the impression is actually a three-dimensional object, use oblique lighting to cast shadows in the valleys and highlights on the peaks of the impression pattern. To do this, hold the camera flash approximately two to three feet away from the impression at about a five to ten degree angle off the ground when taking the photograph.

Figure 7.3   Using straight directional lighting, much of the detail in this shoe print is not visible.

Figure 7.4   Set up your camera on a tripod, making sure the film plane is parallel to the shoe print. Using oblique lighting, shoot three photographs of the shoe print while aiming the flash between the tripod legs.

Making the Cast

Before casting any impression, lightly mist over the entire surface with hair spray or other similar fixative. This will help to keep the fine detail of the impression from being damaged during the casting process. For many years the standard medium for making casts of large impressions was plaster of paris. Because plaster of paris tends to be very fragile, a better substance to use is Traxtone, which was originally created for use by dentists.

Traxtone needs no reinforcement materials as does plaster of paris, and it is easier to mix. It sets in less time than other materials, and it is a much more durable product than plaster of paris. Traxtone comes in pre-measured plastic bags, which, when mixed with water is just about right to cast one shoe print adequately. Pour the entire bag of Traxtone into a large self-sealing bag. Add the correct amount of water specified in the instructions and seal the bag. For your convenience, it is wise to prepare premeasured bottles of water for this mixture. Knead the bag of Traxtone and water until the colored pigments dissolve, indicating that the mixture is ready to use.

To begin casting the impression, start by pouring the Traxtone from the bag just above or below the impression, or whichever part of the impression is on a higher level. Be careful not to pour the mixture directly onto the impression or you may destroy its delicate detail. Allow the mixture to slowly work its way into the impression by pouring slightly behind it. Slowly work the mixture down the entire length of the impression until the

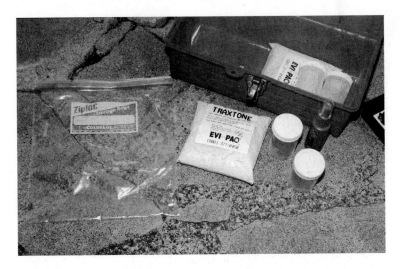

Figure 7.5   This is all that is needed to make a cast using Traxtone.

Figure 7.6 Spray hair spray over the impression to help set it before pouring the cast.

whole impression is completely filled with additional pouring around the outside of the impression as well.

Under normal temperatures, Traxtone will set in approximately twenty minutes, and you will then be able to remove the cast. While waiting for the cast to dry, inscribe onto its surface a NORTH arrow, case number, evidence number, date, time, and your name or distinctive logo. Once

Figure 7.7 Pour the contents of one bag of Traxtone and a premeasured amount of water into a self-sealing bag and mix.

Figure 7.8 Continue mixing until all of the colored pigment indicators are dissolved and the material is a consistent green color.

Figure 7.9 Begin pouring the Traxtone at one end of the impression. If the impression is on a slope, start at the highest end.

Figure 7.10 *Do not* pour directly into the impression. Let the Traxtone flow naturally to avoid damaging the fragile detail. There is no need to build a form around the impression, and no additional supports need to be added to the Traxtone.

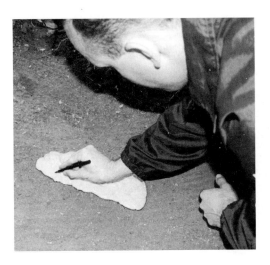

Figure 7.11 Traxtone usually sets within twenty minutes. Make sure to etch in the case number and evidence number to the top side of the cast before it completely dries.

Figure 7.12 Package the cast in a cardboard box like this gun box, making sure the impression side is face up. *Do not* attempt to clean the dirt from the impression in the field.

Figure 7.13 Back at the lab, the cast can be cleaned under running water using a brush. This also allows additional time for the cast to dry. Courtesy of Sheriff's Office, Penobscot County, Maine.

the cast is ready to remove, do so by prying from one side, then securing it in a box with the impression side facing up. This will prevent the impression from damage or wear. Do not attempt to clean dirt or other debris from the cast. That can be done later in the laboratory when the material has dried more thoroughly.

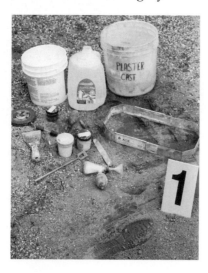

Figure 7.14 These are the tools needed to make a cast using plaster of paris. Courtesy of Sheriff's Office, Penobscot County, Maine.

Figure 7.15 Build a form around the impression to prevent the plaster from flowing out. This will also aid in making the cast thicker, which will add strength to the cast. Courtesy of Sheriff's Office, Penobscot County, Maine.

Plaster of Paris

You will need the following materials: plaster of paris, water, a rubber bowl and spatula for mixing, hair spray or other fixative, thin oil, a syringe, talcum or baby powder, reinforcing materials such as chicken

Figure 7.16 Mix water and plaster of paris in a container until a proper thickness is obtained. Courtesy of Sheriff's Office, Penobscot County, Maine.

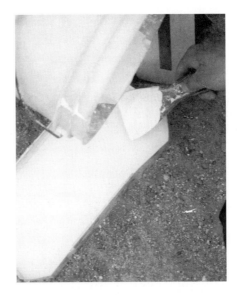

Figure 7.17 Pour the plaster of paris into the mold using a putty knife to break the fall of the plaster as it flows into the mold. Add sticks or pieces of wire to the mold to give it more strength. Courtesy of Sheriff's Office, Penobscot County, Maine.

Figure 7.18 Let the plaster dry. Times may vary depending on temperature and humidity. Etch in the case number and evidence number to the top side of the cast before it completely dries. Courtesy of Sheriff's Office, Penobscot County, Maine.

wire or wooden sticks or cut-up clothes hanger wire, and framing materials such as wood or a corrugated box.

With the wood or corrugated-box material, build a frame around the impression to be cast. Spray the surface with light cooking spray or oil to prevent the plaster from sticking when you pour it. Mix the plaster with water to the thickness of cream, and add salt to hasten the setting process or sugar to slow it down. Slowly pour the mixture over the impression by

Figure 7.19 Carefully lift up the cast from one end. Book the cast in as is. *Do not* attempt to clean the dirt from the impression in the field. Courtesy of Sheriff's Office, Penobscot County, Maine.

using the spatula or a spoon, fork, or putty knife to soften the flow onto the impression to keep it from damaging or destroying the surface. After you have poured about a half inch thickness of the mixture onto the impression, place reinforcing materials onto the surface. Pour more liquid, add more reinforcing materials, then continue filling the area to be cast.

While the plaster is setting, inscribe onto the surface of the cast a NORTH arrow, the case and evidence numbers, the date and time, and your name or distinctive logo.

Water-Filled Impressions

If the impression is in a puddle of water you cannot drain, or if it is in snow, build a frame around the impression and sift dry plaster into the impression until the water is absorbed. Spray fixative from time to time and add reinforcement material as you go. In snow, you may find that spraying with fixative and talcum powder may help preserve the impression before you add the plaster, which has a tendency to heat up as it dries. If you can, drain the impression by cutting a channel from the impression to a lower level, which you may have to dig to allow the water to drain. Let the impression dry, using a turkey baster to help drain out the water, and carefully remove any debris from the surface with tweezers. If you have a power source nearby, you may hasten the drying process with the aid of a hair dryer, not aimed directly at the surface (the air pressure could disturb the surface of the impression). Lightly cover the impression with talcum or baby powder to help soak up some of the moisture, and alternately spray with hair spray or fixative before pouring your casting materials.

Figure 7.20   A rubber bulb or plunger can be used to remove excess water from the impression. Courtesy of Sheriff's Office, Penobscot County, Maine.

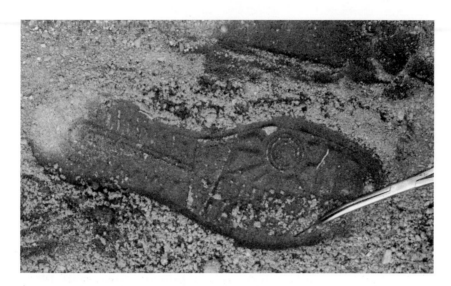

Figure 7.21 Use tweezers, forceps, or a cotton swab to remove debris from the impression. Courtesy of Sheriff's Office, Penobscot County, Maine.

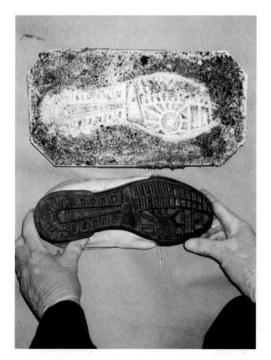

Figure 7.22 Here is a side-by-side comparison of a cast and a suspect shoe showing similar class characteristics. Courtesy of Sheriff's Office, Penobscot County, Maine.

Casting Tool Marks and Small Impressions

Use silicone rubber, latex rubber, microsile, moulage, or one of the compounds that dentists use for making impressions for dentures and other dental prosthetics. Build a frame around the impression to be molded to hold the mixture in and around the impression while it is introduced to the area and until it dries and can be removed intact. Mix the material according to the directions and introduce it to the impression to be cast. As the substance dries, mark the cast with a NORTH arrow, case and evidence numbers, date and time, and your initial or logo. If the object is too small to hold all this information, place it into an envelope and write all the necessary information on the outside of the sealed envelope paper bag or other container rigged to hold the item so that it will not be damaged or destroyed.

If the impression is on a door or window frame or other object that can be removed, do so and take it to the laboratory so that the cast may be made under more ideal conditions away from the crime scene, and at a more convenient time. Casts of the tools suspected of having been used to make the impressions should be made in the laboratory. Photo images of

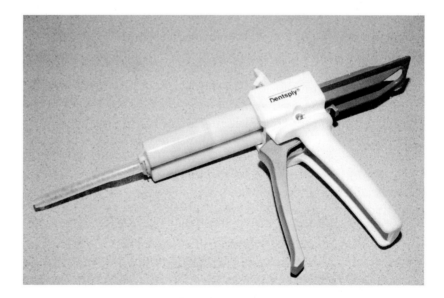

Figure 7.23   This device resembling a caulking gun combines a two-part casting material in a mixing chamber before it is released from the nozzle. This is used for casting gun barrels and other impression evidence. Courtesy of Sheriff's Office, Penobscot County, Maine.

the impressions and tools that possibly made them are studied for similarities and possible matches.

Each tool is unique. Tools are designed differently by the different manufacturers and are made of a wide variety of materials. The metals used for most tools come in different degrees of hardness, depending on their function, quality, and price. New materials are being developed as we speak, such as knives made of porcelain, and some of the old materials are still used, such as rubber and hardwood mallets. Stress and wear eventually cause weaknesses in all tools, and the tools develop cracks, stress fractures, and degeneration from use, time, and the elements.

Whenever two objects come together by pounding, cutting, scraping, prying or rubbing, they mark each other one way or another. The harder material of the two usually makes the mark on the softer material, but some materials mark each other because they have the same hardness quotient. Tools such as hammers and mallets make impressions on the objects they strike; tools used to pry open doors and windows, such as screwdrivers, make impressions on wooden door and window frames; wire cutters used to cut through fences or to cut open padlocks and other tools used to commit crimes leave their signatures on the softer materials. At the same time, the tools themselves undergo changes from such contacts. Wood pried with a screwdriver is going to have to give way to the harder metal object, but in that door or window frame a nail or screw or similar metal object will make marks on the screwdriver. Eventually every tool develops its own distinctive "fingerprint," and then imprints a mirror image of that fingerprint onto the material it strikes, cuts, scrapes, or otherwise impresses as they meet.

When you find a tool suspected of having been used in a crime, photograph it in place, describe it completely in your report, spot its location in your sketch, and handle it carefully, preserving its condition and appearance exactly as you found it. The tool may contain particles of material it was used against, such as wood or metal shavings, blood, hairs, or fibers, so be sure not to clean it off before taking it to the lab for analysis and comparison.

Marks made by tools are called impressions (from pounding or prying) or striations (from scraping). Following are some other tools and the marks they make: A screwdriver makes scrape marks on cash boxes or a cash register; an ice pick may leave scrape marks inside the mechanism when used to open a bathroom door lock. Pipe wrenches leave their marks on pipes, nuts and bolts, doorknobs, and ignition switches. Axes and hatchets leave their signatures on wood, human bones, and skin. Bolt cutters, tin snips, scissors, and shears are used to cut wires, ropes, lock hasps, and sheet metal. Whenever the crime scene search indicates which tools were possibly used, look for those types of tools and take them to the laboratory for comparison and possible matches.

In most cases, the perpetrators will bring along their own tools with which to commit the crime, having prepared themselves for the various obstacles they expect to encounter. When they have completed their work, they take the tools away with them for use another time. Sometimes a burglar will use the same "lucky tools" over and over again, as many other professionals do. As they wear, the tools may chip or leave scrapings behind. The tip of an ice pick found at the crime scene may match the shaft of a pick, or a small chip from the corner of a pry tool may match the broken tool found in the possession of a suspect loitering near the scene.

Some thieves, burglars, and assailants use whatever tools or weapons they find at the crime scene, commit the crime with them, then leave everything but their loot behind so that they will not be caught possessing incriminating tools. It is naturally more difficult to match those tools with their users. When the culprit brings tools to the scene, then leaves them behind, it may be possible to trace their ownership by brand, initials engraved or marks on them, or fingerprints left on the smooth surfaces.

When you find a mark made by the perpetrator using any of the aforementioned tools, or any others we have failed to mention, be sure to photograph them in place first, indicating their exact locations, and describe their appearance in your report. Then follow the procedure for casting the impression described earlier in this chapter. Never place a suspected tool into, onto, or against a mark that was possibly made by that tool, as that would contaminate the evidence. The matches will be made by putting together photos of the corresponding tools and their suspected marks, or by comparing positive and negative molds. Once you touch the suspected tool to the mark it possibly made, you have destroyed their evidentiary value.

Tool marks can and should be measured, but sometimes a tool makes a mark that appears larger or smaller than the tool itself. The reason for this phenomenon is that certain materials, such as wood, stretch under pressure and then retract. The result is that a mark made on a windowsill by a 5/8-inch pry tool may measure out at only 3/8 inch or half inch. Impressions made on other materials, such as sheet metal or aluminum, may stretch and not retract, and the result is that the first examination may indicate that the perpetrator used a larger tool. When you describe the tool and the marks, record your exact measurements. Do not make the mistake of stating "the pry mark was made by a tool with a 5/8-inch bite."

SUMMARY

Do not underestimate the importance of impression evidence no matter how inconsequential it may seem. It is often difficult to recognize such evidence and time-consuming to collect it, but at the time of your investigation it is almost impossible to differentiate between critical and noncritical evidence. Later, when you and your colleagues are putting the case together, you will realize how important such evidence is to the case.

SUGGESTED OUTSIDE PROJECTS

1. Create your own shoe print impressions in different types of soil, such as sand or clay. Practice photographing them with plaster of paris and Traxtone. You will find out which works best for you.

2. Using a variety of hand tools, make your own set of impressions and striation marks in different types of materials. Using different materials, make casts of those impressions.

DISCUSSION QUESTIONS

1. An impression is what form of evidence: physical, trace, or transient?

2. Why take impression photos in black and white instead of color?

3. What are the drawbacks of using plaster of paris?

4. Describe how you would cast a footprint in a mud puddle.

5. What type of mark does a hammer make?

6. How do you light a photograph you are taking of a shoe or tire impression?

7. What is the advantage of using Traxtone instead of plaster of paris?

8. Describe how you would package and transport a cast.

9. What is the difference between a striation and an impression, and describe what type of tool would make each.

10. Why should you *not* place a suspect's shoe into a print left in the mud?

Chapter Eight
Fingerprints

INTRODUCTION

Fingerprints have been, and will continue to be, one of the best forms of identification available to a police investigation. Everyone has fingerprints and footprints, which serve as friction ridges, which are developed on the fetus before birth and remain until after death, barring any catastrophic scarring condition. To date, no two individuals in the world whose fingerprints are on file have ever been found to have the same fingerprints. Identical twins have the same DNA, or genetic code, but not the same fingerprints, so even they have their own unique identities.

In this chapter, we shall cover the types of fingerprints, fingerprint patterns, classification and comparison of fingerprints, places where fingerprints may be found at the crime scene, and the different techniques used to develop fingerprints.

THE FINGERPRINT EXPERT

As a trained crime scene investigator, you may or may not be qualified as a fingerprint expert. In this text we are operating on the assumption that you are qualified as an expert only in identifying, collecting, and preserving evidence. Other texts will address the expert qualification requirements. As with photography and other aspects of crime scene investigation, you should be careful to avoid representing yourself as an expert if you are not, as some attorneys are very talented in bursting the bubbles of officers who exaggerate their qualifications. In order to be able to collect and preserve fingerprints efficiently for the expert in the laboratory, you do not have to be able to analyze and compare prints. You will, however, be expected to have sufficient knowledge to develop good prints for the expert, and to roll prints of suspects and others for elimination purposes.

What Are Fingerprints?

The skin on the surfaces of the hands and feet comes equipped with built-in ridges, known as friction ridges, that enable the person to hold objects and to stand without his or her hands and feet slipping. Without these ridges, standing and holding objects would be far more difficult. Even simple tasks such as unscrewing the cap off a mayonnaise jar would be far more difficult than it is now with the aid of those ridges. The skin is an organ of the body that consists of two layers. The top or outer layer is called the epidermis and contains the friction ridges. Beneath the epidermis is the dermis, which is joined together by the dermal papillae. Deep in the dermis layer are the sweat glands and sweat gland ducts. These sweat ducts go up through the dermis to the epidermis, where they form sweat pores along the ridges. Throughout the day sweat comes out through the pores and onto the surface of the skin and along the ridges. Sweat consists of water, salts, oils, amino acids, fatty acids, and other materials that come from objects the hands or feet touch. When you touch an object, fingerprints are transferred onto the surface with the sweat and other materials in the pattern of the ridges in pretty much the same way that images are printed with printers' ink.

Because the printed images of the ridges are made with the nearly invisible sweat materials, they are hard to see with the naked eye. These nearly invisible prints are called latent prints, obviously because they have to be made visible with the aid of chemicals, powders, digital or photo image enhancement, and sometimes ultraviolet or infrared lighting. At the typical crime scene, if one can be considered "typical," you will have to develop these "latent" prints to make them visible so that you may collect them for identification purposes.

The second type of print is the patent print. Unlike the latent print, the patent print is visible to the naked eye. This is usually because certain materials, such as paint, grease, oil, ink, or blood is picked up by the friction ridges, mixed with the sweat, and printed onto the surfaces the person touches.

Next is the plastic print. This print is three-dimensional and the individual has touched some type of pliable substrate such as putty, wax, chocolate, or grease. It will be difficult to collect these by transferring onto tape as you collect the other prints, and you should photograph them before making any attempt to remove them from any surface.

The fourth type of print is the inked print. An inked print is made by applying a thin layer of black printers' ink onto the surface of the friction skin and transferring its impressions onto a card, paper, or other document to preserve as a permanent record. An example of an inked print would be one that you have placed onto a "ten print" fingerprint card designed for use to record fingerprints of suspects, job applicants, and other people legitimately at a crime scene for "elimination prints," or to eliminate their prints found at the scene because they had a legitimate reason for leaving their prints there, such as being residents and guests. These prints are used for documentation, classification, comparison, and importation into a computer database as a permanent record. Unknown prints will be compared against various databases in an effort to identify their owners.

If you come across a scene that is completely devoid of any prints, either you have a scene untouched by human hands or feet, including those of the victims and other inhabitants of the premises, or you have a scene that has been carefully wiped clean of all prints in an effort to hide the identity of the perpetrators. In spite of all the publicity about how valuable prints are to criminal investigations, many offenders do leave their prints behind. Some perpetrators do not plan their crimes well or are interrupted by returning victims or the police, and they do not have time to think about their prints. Some criminals, believe it or not, do not even consider the possibility of being caught and are very sloppy, leaving evidence all over the place. Some criminals simply do not think. Still others will automatically assume that a witness will remain silent and cover for them because of some real or imagined bond between the witness and the perpetrator. Very close friends, relatives, or colleagues are known to develop a code of silence. That is one reason why some perpetrators are nonchalant about leaving evidence scattered all over the place.

When searching for prints, be sure to include palm and footprints, even though your agency and most others do not have classification systems for those types of prints on file. When you locate a suspect, the fingerprint expert in the lab may be able to make positive pattern matches of inked prints of suspects produced in the laboratory and those lifted at the crime scenes because of the unique characteristics of those prints.

Before processing any surface for latent prints, carefully examine the surface to make a decision as to which method you will use for developing and collecting any prints you might find. For example, porous items such as paper or cardboard can often be better processed in the laboratory using chemicals such as iodine, ninhydrin, or other physical developer. On nonporous surfaces, such as glass or metal, the basic black powder may be the best medium to use. Of course, whenever it is possible to move an object bearing a print, it is wise to take it to the lab for processing. For example, cyanoacrylate ester, also known as Super Glue, can be used in a specially constructed airtight chamber. In the field, powders are usually the medium of choice for processing prints.

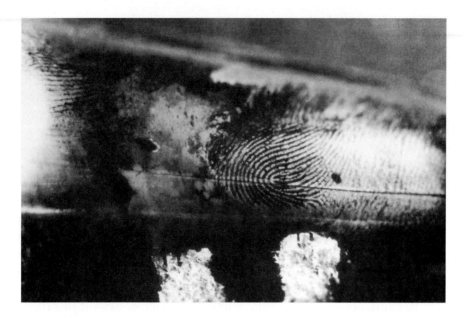

Figure 8.1 This fingerprint was developed using cyanoacrylate ester or Super Glue. Notice how the fingerprint turns white. At this point the fingerprint can be photographed or developed more with powders or dye staining.

Search all surfaces where one might have touched during the commission of the particular crime you are investigating, and even places where it would not seem logical that someone would touch. Use a strong light and shine it obliquely across the surface to see if you can detect any disturbance of dust on polished surfaces, or traces of prints. Then use the brush and powder of a color that contrasts with the color of the host surface you are dusting. While black powder is the most common, you will usually have a variety of colors and types of powders to use. The best host surfaces for fingerprints will be smooth and nonporous materials, but always try to get prints off of any object that the perpetrator may have touched. New discoveries are made every once in a while, such as prints on skin, certain cloth materials, and other surfaces heretofore not even attempted to take prints from.

Dusting for Prints

Having selected the appropriate powder and your favorite brush, begin brushing lightly over an area where you believe you might find a latent print. First, picture in your mind how and where a person might have touched that particular object, and move your brush across the imaginary

Figure 8.2   A basic black powder kit consists of black powder, an application brush, lifting tape, white lift cards, and a portable ink pad.

print until you have laid down a smooth field of powder. If nothing appears, move on to the next probable area location and repeat the process.

From a public relations standpoint, there are two considerations here. First, you must appear as though you know what you are doing and your approach will make that impression. Second, consider the victim's property. The place may have been "trashed" by the burglar or vandal. But you need not add to the victim's loss by spilling fingerprint powder all over

Figure 8.3   Use a flashlight at an oblique angle to locate disruptions in the dust and/or to visualize fingerprints.

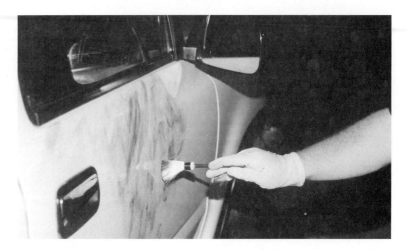

Figure 8.4 Apply a thin layer of black powder to the surface. Once fingerprints are visualized, slowly continue dusting the print until it is fully developed. Do not overpowder your evidence.

the place. Use the powder sparingly, and when you are dusting a space on a wall, tape a card or paper to the wall below the place you are dusting, then fold up the two free corners of the card or paper to the wall, making a dustpan of sorts. This is particularly important when you are working in a room with a deep shag carpet of a very light color. Even when you are careful, it will take several vacuum attempts to clean up after you leave.

When you find a print, brush lightly along the same direction as the emerging ridges, with the objective to bring out the entire pattern or patterns of the prints, and at the same time reducing the amount of powder that has accumulated between the ridges. Now that you have revealed at least one print, expand your search area for additional latents that you might develop.

It is a good practice to photograph all prints before you attempt to lift them. This applies as well to the visible (or patent) and plastic prints, as you may destroy a print while lifting it from the surface. The fingerprint technician in the lab will at least have the photograph to work with. Use the fingerprint camera, making sure that the print and the film are parallel so as to avoid distorting an enlargement of the image.

Lifting the Print

Now that you have photographed the print, examine it carefully to see if it can be transferred to transparent adhesive tape. If it is a plastic print in a gummy substance, such as partially dried paint or grease, you may not be able to transfer it onto the tape. That's why you photographed it first. If you cannot transfer the impression, see if there is some way to remove

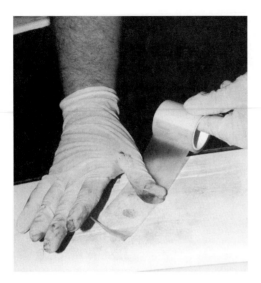

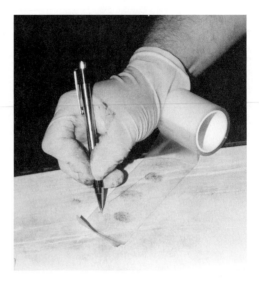

Figure 8.5 Lay down lifting tape over the print, starting at one end and then smoothing it out over the entire surface with your finger. Be sure to smooth out the tape to remove all air bubbles.

Figure 8.6 Once the tape is in place, draw an up arrow on the tape to help with orientation later. Be careful not to draw over the fingerprint.

the host object, such as a chair or table, or even a window frame or a door, depending on the importance of the print to the investigation.

Use transparent tape free of bubbles and wide enough to cover the entire print you intend to lift. If you have several prints together, plan the placement of the tape so that the edge of the tape does not end on the middle of a print. It is going to be difficult to put two strips of tape side by side to get an undisturbed print. Keep your own fingers off the sticky side of the tape that is going to lay on top of the print(s). Slowly and steadily pull the length of tape that you are going to use without stopping so as to avoid leaving an accumulation of adhesive on the sticky side of the tape, which will interfere with the pattern of the print.

Attach the loose end of the tape to the surface at least an inch beyond the print you are going to lift. Then carefully lay the tape down smoothly and evenly, keeping it extended so that the magnetic characteristics of the tape do not cause it to attach itself to the surface unevenly. Continue applying and smoothing the tape onto the surface until you have laid it down at least one inch beyond the print you intend to lift. Use a plastic ruler or your fingernail to smooth out the bubbles. Instead of rubbing the tape where you cannot make the tape stick to the surface, puncture the bubble with the tip of an X-acto knife and then press the tape to the surface.

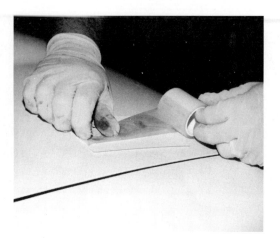

Figure 8.7   Slowly peel the lifting tape off starting at one end. Keep your hand on the other end so the tape does not stick to itself.

Figure 8.8   Apply the tape to the finger-print lift card in the same way, starting at one end and working it down to the other end to prevent air bubbles in the tape.

Carefully and slowly remove the tape, which is now holding the impression transferred from the host surface. Keep the tape extended so that it will not double up and attach to itself and destroy the print that is now on it. Place a white card, or one of a contrasting color if you are not using black powder, on a flat surface so that it will not move. Check to make sure that the card will hold the entire transferred print. Attach the edge of the tape that does not contain any of the transferred print onto the edge of the card and roll the entire length of the tape onto the card. Instead of cards, your agency may use transparent plastic sheets to hold the transferred prints.

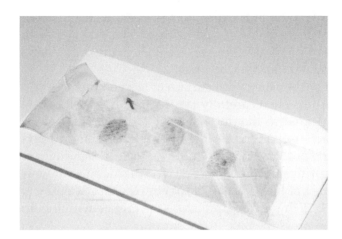

Figure 8.9   Once the lift is completed, fill out the other side of the card with a detailed description of where the print was obtained, the date, time, case number, as well as your name and badge number.

Figure 8.10   Using a pocket inker, apply a thin layer of black ink to the entire surface of the subject's finger.

Rolling the Exemplar, or "Elimination," Print

Whenever you find fingerprints and other prints at the crime scene, your objective is to identify who put them there. Although you may actually fingerprint the perpetrator, you will be rolling prints on everyone who possibly left prints at the crime scene, which will include victims, witnesses, guests, and other people who had access to the premises. The fingerprint technician in the lab will check the prints found at the scene with prints on file of your colleagues who may have touched something during the investigation. The purpose of the elimination printing process is to take innocent persons off the list of possible suspects in the case. In the process it is not unusual that at least one of them cannot be eliminated, and that person turns out to be a suspect.

Figure 8.11   Start with the right thumb and work your way down to the little finger. Make sure to roll the print to get as much of the fingerprint detail as possible onto the card.

Figure 8.12   Label the fingers 1 through 10 starting with the right thumb as number 1 down to the right little finger and then the left thumb as number 6 down to the left little finger.

At your department, the fingerprint laboratory will have a special setup for fingerprinting people. On the counter will be a glass plane that you will coat with a thin layer of printers' ink, and there will be a device to hold the fingerprint cards in place. In the field you will have ink pads and a portable fingerprinting outfit with a flat surface and holder for the fingerprint cards. The fingerprint cards will be printed with spaces designating all ten digits and at the bottom will be spaces for the thumbs separately and all four fingers together. If you do not have printed fingerprint cards, plain cards will do. All you have to do is label each digit that you print.

Place the ink pad and card holder on a table or other flat surface at about elbow height. Direct the subject to stand behind and slightly to your right with his or her right hand extended so that you can use your left hand for rolling the fingers separately on the ink pad and then onto the card in sequence. With your right hand, straighten out each finger as you ink and roll it, and fold the other fingers inward toward the palm out of the way. Direct the subject to relax and to let you guide the hands and fingers as you go through the procedure. An uncooperative subject or one with arthritis will be difficult to print. Do not stop the procedure until you have a complete set of legible prints. After you complete the individual thumbs and fingers, there are spaces for each thumb and all four fingers of each hand. You do not roll these. Press the thumbs one at a time onto the ink pad and then onto the card. When you print all four fingers of each hand, place them flat onto the ink pad, then guide them onto the card so that all four fingers lie flat on the card. You may have to turn the hand slightly so that the little finger will also print the card.

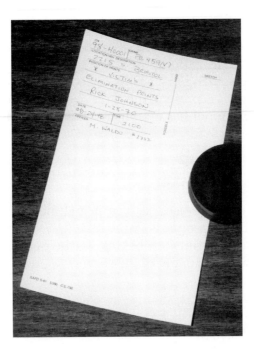

Figure 8.13 Fill out the back of the card with the subject's name, case number, date, and time, as well as your name and badge number.

When you roll each thumb and finger separately, be sure to ink all of the digit by rolling the entire friction ridge surface, about 180 degrees. The secret is to practice so that you use just the right amount of ink and pressure to ink the digits without filling the spaces between the ridges with ink. Then use the same amount of pressure as you place each digit onto the card, and you will make a legible print. If you accidentally smudge a print, start again until all prints are clear and legible. If a digit is missing, write in "missing" in the space where the missing digit would have been printed.

Palm and Footprints

Select a card or paper large enough to hold the entire impression. Ink the entire surface of the foot or palm by rolling the ink onto the surface with a roller, or use an even pressure on the foot or palm while applying the ink, and again while printing the impression onto the card or paper. You can also use this procedure for making impressions of shoes or socks. Instruct the person to wear the item while you apply the ink, then have him or her step evenly onto the paper to print the impression. Be sure to have the subject remove the inked footwear after making the imprint so that you can avoid having ink all over the place.

Printing Deceased or Unconscious Persons

The fingerprint technician will handle these procedures in the hospital or the morgue using a field kit. Decomposed bodies may actually require removing the fingers and soaking in a hardening solution before trying to roll the prints. If rigor mortis is present, the rigor may be broken only after the coroner or medical examiner has established the time of death.

SUMMARY

Fingerprints will continue to be used as a principal means of positively identifying people. For that reason it is imperative that you meticulously search every crime scene for prints left behind by the perpetrators, even though you will not find any at many of the scenes.

SUGGESTED OUTSIDE PROJECTS

1. Practice rolling exemplar prints of your friends or fellow students until you are able to produce clean and legible print cards.

2. Touch various types of host surfaces with your bare hands, dust for prints and lift them, then transfer them onto white cards as described in the chapter.

DISCUSSION QUESTIONS

1. When it comes to twins, why are fingerprints better for identification purposes?

2. What is the purpose for taking "elimination prints"?

3. What is a latent print, and how do you develop it for collection?

4. What is a plastic print?

5. Explain the procedure for dusting an area for prints.

6. Is it possible to identify a perpetrator with palm prints?

7. What parts of the body contain friction ridges?

8. Explain the procedure for rolling exemplar, or elimination, prints.

9. Why should you photograph prints before lifting them?

10. What is the likelihood of two people in this country having identical fingerprints?

Chapter Nine
Documenting the Crime:
Reports, Photographs, Videos, and Sketches

INTRODUCTION

Once you have left the crime scene and you are on your way back to the office with your evidence collection, you will probably never have a chance to go back and repeat the investigation. Even when you have the luxury of returning to an undisturbed scene for a second time and to retrace your steps from beginning to end, picking up loose ends and discovering crucial evidence that you missed the first (or second or third) time, it will never be the same. There will be critics who will suggest that you went back to change evidence, or—worse yet—that you planted evidence.

Your reports, sketches, photographs, and videotapes should reinforce one another in reconstructing the entire investigation from beginning to end. Your reports will show the sequential developments of your role in the investigation process. If you could have the entire investigation video-taped from beginning to end, your written report should be almost like a transcript of the event. The photographs will show the overall scene, and then a series of photos will take the viewer on a tour through the scene, showing the dimensions and relationships of the evidence to the various other objects encountered during the investigation. Your sketch will serve as a blueprint for re-creation of the scene exactly as you found it upon your arrival. Together, all of these tools will guide all the other people involved in the investigation to a successful conclusion. Eventually they should aid in presentation of the evidence in court.

THE REPORT

In this chapter we will be dealing only with your reports as a crime scene investigator. For more information on the overall reports, including the original crime report, interviewing victims and witnesses, and other follow-up reports, see *Police Field Operations*, fourth edition.[1] The report should be a step-by-step account of exactly who was involved in the search; what role each of the participants played in the investigation; what evidence was found, by whom; and what was done with each item of evidence from the moment it was picked up and prepared for transportation to the office or the laboratory, how it was handled enroute and by whom, and what time it was at each step along the way.

A voice-actuated microcassette recorder is probably the best piece of equipment to use for accurately recording your notes that you will later put in written form at the office. A notebook or clipboard and pen will get in the way when you are taking photographs and collecting and packaging evidence. You can put the recorder in a shirt pocket or hang it around your neck. You should record a running dialogue, documenting what you are doing, what you and your colleagues find, what you do not find, including your observations of other people at the scene, what they are saying, and generally every part of your investigation as it moves along.

Begin your report by entering all of the identifying data of yourself and your colleagues. If this is a standardized report form supplied by your department, it will have spaces for filling in all the essential information. Date and time of the crime, time of your arrival and departure, classification of the crime, and other essential data are recorded. You should also describe the lighting and weather conditions, the temperature, and any other information relevant to the case. You may be required by your department to start off your report with a brief summary of your investigation followed by an itemized list of evidence. Actually, this is a good practice, because it gives the prosecutor a thumbnail sketch of the status of the investigation and an idea of how to proceed with the prosecution. Follow-up investigators and supervisors may read only the summary to refresh their memories instead of having to read the entire report again.

Record your first observations of the overall scene upon your arrival, the names and specific duty assignments of other officers at the scene, and especially the exact location and description of the property. An example might be: "A wood frame two-story house with an attached two-car garage in the center of a one-acre lot on the southwest corner of Sixteenth and Spruce." An example of a business address might be: "Suite 318, a six-room suite taking up the entire south half of the third floor in an eight-story concrete and brick office building located approximately midblock on the north side of Chatway Street, address 1353." List the names or

[1]Thomas F. Adams, *Police Field Operations*, 4th ed. (Upper Saddle River, NJ: Prentice Hall, 1998).

descriptions of people milling about the scene, and indicate whether the crime scene has been defined by barricades or warning tape, or by officers protecting the scene from contamination.

Record everything you see, hear, taste, feel, and smell. Although many of those sensory experiences will not be considered of any evidentiary value, they may be useful to the officer assigned to the initial investigation or the follow-up investigators. Working on your theory of transference, record also what you do not find that one would normally expect to find. For example, one would expect to find fingerprints in a room occupied by people, but your search yields absolutely none, indicating that someone must have wiped them clean. You may see several nails or hooks on a wall with nothing hanging from them, or a knife rack missing a knife that you do not find anywhere on the premises. Your tour guide may point out to you the presence of certain tools or other items that were not in place before the crime, such as a screwdriver that does not belong to the occupant of the house, which is an example of transference.

The Search

Describe the room or area that you searched, its dimensions and general appearance, and who did the searching. Instead of stating something like "the undersigned searched . . . " or "officers searched . . . " or "Officer Villis and I searched the entire scene," record exactly what Officer Villis searched and what you searched. When something is found, report who found it and where, describing its condition and location. If a witness finds an item and turns it over to you, say so, and be sure to get the name of the witness and where you might find him or her later. It will not go over big in court if you say something like "it was found" or "an unknown person handed me the item and he said he found it on the living room floor next to the sofa." In the infamous O. J. Simpson case, criminalist Dennis Fung of the LAPD Crime Lab testified, "I collected the samples," when actually it was not he, but his junior partner who collected the samples. Sometimes an officer may erroneously say, "An item of evidence was found." "*Who* found what?" the judge will demand. Such errors ruin your credibility.

Evidence

Describe each item of evidence as thoroughly as you can, including its appearance and condition, such as "wet stains which appeared to be blood" or "bloodstains on the bedsheet covering the bed in the master bedroom where the victim stated the rape took place." If you state that the stains were blood, then add a statement as to how you determined it was blood if there might be any doubt, such as by a benzedine test. Otherwise your statement should be that the stains *appeared* to be blood. If you find shoe prints in a mud puddle, and you drain the water so as to make a cast of the impression, report that you drained the water, and how you did it. Then describe the procedure you went through to photograph the impression and make a cast of the print.

Be precise in your report as to exactly who found the evidence, who made the cast, who collected the evidence and how, who packaged the evidence and how, and any other information to document the evidence collection procedure completely. After the evidence was packaged, your report should then continue with the journey of that evidence to its final destination in the lab or evidence locker. You must deal with each item of evidence in this same careful manner with great attention to detail. The integrity of your investigation and reports depends on it.

Sequence

The sequence of your report should parallel the sequence of your investigation. You are taking the reader on a tour through the crime scene in the same sequence as when you went through it. The principal crime report prepared by the officer originally assigned to the case may be laid out to show how the crime is likely to have taken place with a hypothetical sequence, but your report should reflect the sequence of your investigation. Later, when you are putting your notes together to prepare your report, you will also prepare a summary statement to explain everything you did at the scene, such as collection of so many items of evidence, casting tool marks, sketching the scene, taking fourteen Polaroid photos, videotaping the scene, and taking eighty-seven photographs.

Next, your list of evidence should be laid out so that the other people involved in the investigation and eventual prosecution of the case will have a complete list of evidence at their fingertips. For example, your evidence list should start like this:

1. Latent fingerprints found in living room, #5, 9, 14.

2. Man's white shirt and light blue pants found on floor in master bedroom saturated with what appears to be dried blood, #27, 28 (sizes and brands, if indicated).

3. Plaster casts of two shoe prints found in the mud below and outside the front window on the northwest side of the house, the point of entry; both prints appear to have been made by shoes of the same size, #2, 3.

4. And so forth, listing all evidence.

The numbers should correspond with photograph numbers and also be located and numbered in your sketch. Describe each item so that it will not be confused with other evidence of a similar nature.

Chain of Custody

After you have listed all the items of evidence, present in your report an account of the journey and destination of each item. To save space and to assure accuracy, you may wish to include the numbers you have designated to each item in your summary. For example: "Items 37 through 42 and 64 through 110 were taken to the evidence lab for analysis and handed to criminalist Mr. P. Sorvino. All other items numbered as follows . . . were placed in the evidence room accepted and logged by B. Pearlman, supervisor of Evidence Custody." Some items may be sent directly to laboratories out of state, such as the FBI and Cell-Mark. Report who sent the packages and by what means, such as Federal Express, and when you receive the return receipts or verifications of receipt, report the name of the persons who signed for the objects at those labs.

Corpus Delicti

The primary officer assigned to investigate the crime is responsible for explaining all of the elements of the corpus delicti that can be proven by testimony and evidence to justify the crime report. Your crime scene investigation report should demonstrate that all the evidence essential to the corpus delicti has been collected in accordance with the existing statutes, case law, and the Constitution. A perpetrator who breaks into a building and is caught before he or she can steal anything is still guilty of burglary in some states, but because there is no evidence of the perpetrator actually stealing or committing a felony, the prosecutor may decline to prosecute for anything other than misdemeanor vandalism or trespassing. The basis for rejection is that without evidence of more than mere entry, a jury would probably not find the defendant guilty of the more serious felony. Sometimes the more serious crime has been committed, but sloppy or incomplete investigations fail to produce the evidence necessary to sustain the charges. Be careful that you do not fall into the "sloppy" or "incomplete" categories.

Reporting Your Photographs

When you took photographs, you numbered or lettered them sequentially, or used some other method to separate them from items of evidence. List the photos in sequence and describe what each one is expected to depict. Your report should also include a statement that your sketch, if you made one, includes a symbol and number (or letter) representing where the camera was placed and in what direction it was aimed. You should briefly describe the type of camera that you used, but because you do not intend to represent yourself as an expert, do not go into detail about film and lens and other matters that you are not expected to know. All you have to do is testify that you took the pictures and that they represent the scene you saw in person. If you are a photo expert, be prepared to spend a lot of your time under cross-examination in an effort to discredit you by insinuating what you might have done in the darkroom to make the photos show what you wanted to show. Even if you are an expert, we suggest that you don't supply information unless the prosecutor asks for it.

Sketches

If you or another officer draw one or more sketches, include that information in your report. You will probably be the one to draw the rough sketch, and a draftsperson or architect from the public works or city engineer's office may later prepare a detailed drawing. In your report, be sure to describe how the sketch ties in with the photographs and other items of evidence. Make certain that all the numbers and letters match so that when you refer to evidence number thirty-four it is not confused with a photograph number thirty-four.

Statements of Others

As we said earlier in this chapter, your primary role is to investigate the crime scene and to leave questioning witnesses and victims to the primary officer on the case. However, while you are doing your work, if you overhear conversations between witnesses or suspects, or if the victim talks with you about the crime, be sure to prepare a supplemental report for the follow-up investigators that covers all the information you gleaned from those conversations. Do not take it for granted that another officer will get the same information. To include information such as this in your crime scene report would dilute the value of the CSI report.

PHOTOGRAPHING THE SCENE

Keep an accurate log of all photographs you take and keep a separate numbering system for each camera you use, such as 35mm, SLR, Polaroid, digital, fingerprint, and any others. Whenever you take a photograph, place a symbol in your sketch at the location from which you took each picture and the compass direction you aimed the camera. In your photo

Figure 9.1   Numbered placards are used to identify pieces of evidence within the crime scene.

log, describe what it is that the photo is expected to depict. When you eventually have the photos developed and arranged in sequence, it is possible that some of them will not come out clearly or in focus or are in some other way unacceptable to present in court as evidence. Do not discard those, but include them along with the others. When asked by the follow-up investigators, or the prosecutor, or even the defense attorneys during discovery proceedings or at the trial, you will have the bad photos to show and it will be obvious why you did not use them. If you discard the bad shots, someone

Figure 9.2   Mid-range photographs are important to identify an item of evidence.

may say that you just destroyed those photos that did not help your case. A rule of evidence is that evidence suppressed is presumed to have been suppressed for a reason, the reason being that perhaps it helps the other side, in this case the defense. Let the other side see for itself that what you did was simply take a bad picture.

Selecting Camera Equipment

Your duty assignment in the department may not require or even allow you to have anything to do with selection of the equipment you use as a crime scene investigator. Our view is that if you are responsible for using the equipment you should have something to say about selecting it. You need quality equipment to produce good results. "You do not find quality very often in the bargain basement" is an apropos slogan when it comes to crime investigation equipment. Your cameras need to be capable of taking pictures of better than snapshot quality, which means that the lens must be of good quality, free of distortion with no imperfections. Stay out of the seconds store. The film should be fast enough to capture the picture in sometimes less than ideal lighting conditions, and the flash should be bright enough to illuminate the scene. You will also need additional lighting equipment to fill in the shadows where necessary.

Digital cameras may be in your arsenal, because the prices are more manageable for government agencies. There are many advantages to digital photography, as the experts will tell you. If you are qualified and trained as an expert, then you will be the person delegated the responsibility to choose the best equipment for your needs. You will also need the fingerprint camera and the Polaroid.

Start each crime scene with new rolls of film for all of the cameras that you use. The photos are not likely to get mixed up with scenes from other crimes, and the picture numbers will correspond more closely with your numbering system for the crime you are currently investigating.

What to Photograph

Obviously, each crime scene is different and will require a modified approach, depending on time of day, weather conditions, available light, equipment on hand, type of crime, and how much time you have to conduct the investigation. The crime may be indoors or outdoors or both. It may be a traffic collision, an arson, a robbery, a burglary, a criminal homicide, or any of a number of crimes against persons or property. Following are a few general rules for photographing most crime scenes.

1. You want to take orientation shots of the location where the event occurred. When you watch a television show or movie,

you first see a view of the outside of the building before you go to the scene inside the apartment, or the outside of the precinct station before the scene shifts to the detective division office on the second floor. These "orientation shots" show the viewer the general location of the crime, starting with the street signs at the intersection, then the view from the corner down the street to focus on the house or building where the crime took place. Next, the front of the building, the entrance, the point of entry, if different than the customary method of entry, the hallway leading to the room or rooms where the actual crime occurred, and a view of each room from the door looking in.

2. Introduce the viewer to each room or area where the crime took place. The first picture will be from the doorway, then from each compass point, moving in a clockwise course. In your sketch, show the location of the camera, sequence of photographs, and direction the camera was pointed for each photo. While you are rotating around the room and taking general overview shots and significant objects are in the picture, such as a victim's body or a broken window, move in on the object and take another picture before you move on to the next location. If you are using a camcorder for your orientation tour, zoom in and back out as you focus on crucial objects to show the viewer approximately where the object is located in relationship to the rest of the room.

3. Take close-up shots of each item of evidence in place as you find it and before touching or attempting to remove it. If you are working with a partner, one of you should take the photos while the other leads the search and identifies each object as it is found and photographed. You should decide beforehand how you are going to divide the workload, including making the photo log. If you search a second time, reverse roles so that one of you may find something that the other one may have overlooked.

4. After you have completed photographing everything that you intended to, go back and retrace your steps. Take additional photos of items that you consider extremely important, perhaps from a different angle or with a different f-stop, shutter speed, and lighting. Your objective is to get clear, high-contrast photos that show each item of evidence in detail. You are

not aiming for portraits, but you want to depict the scene and the objects in it exactly as they appear to your naked eye while you are taking the photos. This second time around, if you have the time, you may see objects differently than you did the first time, perhaps because of ambient lighting or a serial number on an object that you did not see from a different angle. Be sure to catalog these photos to correspond with the photos of the same scene or object the first time around. For example, photos 67 and 68 may be of the same piece of evidence as photos 34 and 35, but from a new perspective. All four of those photos may enhance your presentation of the case better than just the first two by themselves.

5. After you have finished your crime scene investigation and packaged all the evidence for transportation back to the office, take a few additional shots of the other investigators and bystanders, perhaps using just a snapshot camera, to help you later remember the faces you saw while you were working at the scene. You may need to go back and get elimination fingerprints and shoe prints of some of those people, so that their prints may be separated from those of the perpetrator. It is also possible, as we mentioned earlier, that the perpetrator might have returned to the scene to check up and see how the investigation was going. Sometimes a review of photos from several crime scenes may show one or two faces that seem to be at every burglary you investigate. It could be mere coincidence, or you might have a picture of the perpetrator.

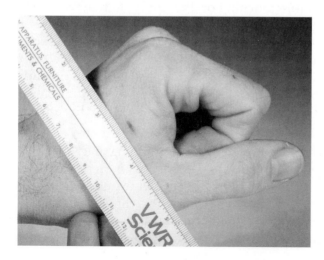

Figure 9.3 Close-up photographs should always be taken with a scale.

Figure 9.4   Oblique lighting across this blank piece of paper reveals what was written on the paper above it in a notepad.

Basic Guidelines for Taking Photographs

Whenever you take close-up photos of evidence items, such as weapons, tools, prints, or other traces, place a ruler or evidence tag with a ruler printed along the edge of the tag. In the darkroom you or the person who develops the photos can adjust the image projected onto the print paper with another ruler in the darkroom so that the ruler in the photo and the ruler you place on the projected image are superimposed so that you will be able to develop the picture to show the actual size of the piece of evidence. This is known as a 1 : 1 photo. This may be very critical, especially if you want to demonstrate that a tool was exactly three-quarters of an inch wide at the tip and the mark probably made by that tool is approximately three-quarters of an inch wide, allowing for the elasticity of the wood in which the impression was made.

When photographing charred or burnt objects, remember to adjust the camera and the lighting to compensate for the absorption of light by the dark surface. Also, to get a profile shot of the surface of burnt wood, shoe prints, or fingerprints, try taking a shot or two with the overhead lighting subdued, and use an oblique light that will make ridges and depressions in the material to look more like hills and valleys, illustrating the detail of the surface more graphically.

PRESENTATION OF PHOTOGRAPHS IN COURT

Bring with you all the photographs you took at the scene and the negatives. You should be able to account for every single numbered shot that you took, although you may show only some of those photos. You must have them, however, for discovery purposes and to refute any claim that you did not bring photographs that were favorable to the defense. You and the prosecutor will go over which photos you should present and in what sequence. This will be very simple for you if you kept an accurate log. Sometimes the court will not allow certain gruesome or graphic photos of the victim because it would tend to incite or inflame the jury, causing jury members to render a verdict based on a skewed emotional attitude rather than on the facts presented to them.

When you present the photographs while on the witness stand, your testimony should be about who took the pictures, when, and where, to lay the foundation. Then you will be asked if they fairly represent what you saw at the scene while taking the pictures. You may be asked to present the negatives to prove that you did not do anything in the development process to change the images. One reason why you do not want to represent yourself as an expert (unless the prosecutor insists that you do) is that experts can play tricks in the darkroom, such as removing a face from the picture, or superimposing the face of someone who was nowhere around when the photos were shot. A sharp defense attorney may sow the seed of doubt in the minds of at least one juror that someone falsified the evidence in some way. Testify honestly and thoroughly and let the attorneys fight it out.

SKETCHING THE SCENE

Along with the photograph and the report, the sketch is third of your trilogy of tools to take the observer back to the crime scene to see it as it presented itself to you. The sketch you will produce most frequently will be your *rough sketch*, which is the easiest to make. You may make this sketch in the field with a pen, graph paper (or regular unlined paper), and a ruler. You may have more sophisticated drawing instruments with you, but you will probably use them to prepare a more detailed sketch later in the office, after you have left the crime scene and deposited all of your evidence appropriately and while you are preparing your report.

Types of Sketches

1. *Locality sketch.* This is an overall view of the scene and its environs, including neighboring buildings, roads leading to the scene, and the location of the crime or collision in relationship to the surrounding landmarks. What you are doing here is drawing a map similar to one that you will find on a college campus or in a large building that pinpoints the place

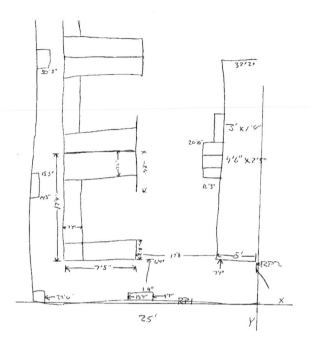

Figure 9.5   Here is a rough sketch taken at a crime scene with the necessary measurements included.

where you are standing and labels it *"You are here."* In your sketch, use a star or arrow to pinpoint the exact location of the crime scene.

2. *Grounds sketch.* Make a grounds sketch when your objective is to show the collision or crime scene in context with its general surroundings. A grounds sketch would show where the collision occurred, including the skid marks, the location where the vehicles were located when the drivers first knew the collision was going to take place (the "point of awareness"), the skid marks, the point of impact, and the final resting place of the vehicles. This sketch should also show the traffic controls, the streets and nearest intersection, view obstructions, and lighting devices, all critical to the investigation. If the crime was committed outdoors, the grounds sketch would show the street or road, and other identifiable landmarks for reference, such as a tennis court, barn, or house, location of any lights (if any), entrances to the area, driveways, pathways, or parking lots in the immediate vicinity of where the crime occurred.

3. *Building sketch.* This is similar to the grounds sketch, except that it is an interior view. For example, if a robbery occurred

in a convenience market, you should sketch the entire building, indicating the location of the convenience market relative to the other businesses in the same building. The sketch should include the entire unit showing the main sales room where the crime took place and a general floor plan of the entire unit, including doors and windows.

4. *Location sketch.* The location sketch shows the total crime scene, as marked off with warning tapes or barricades, excluding the surrounding neighborhood as in the locality sketch. If an entire house is involved in a crime, such as a burglary where the perpetrators ransacked the entire house, this sketch will be the same as a building sketch, supplemented by one or more detailed sketches where the evidence is located.

5. *Detailed sketch.* This is a close-up view of the immediate scene by itself, such as the room or rooms where the actual crime took place. For this sketch, you are "zooming in" so that you can show the locations where evidence has been found and provide a blueprint for the reconstruction of the crime scene. When you draw a detailed sketch of one room at a time, you should consider drawing it in the "cross-projection" mode. To

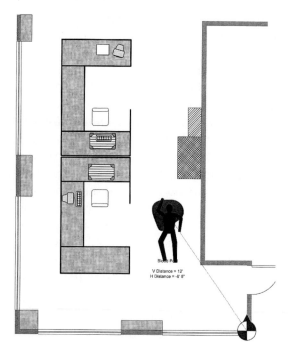

Figure 9.6 Final diagram using a computer-based crime scene diagram program.

do the cross-projection, draw the walls folded down as you would fold down the sides of a box, giving the viewer a multidimensional view of the room by sketching evidence found on the floor and also critical evidence in the walls, such as bullet holes, and doors and windows, such as pry marks or broken glass. You are looking down from the ceiling, which makes it possible to present the sketch in three dimensions.

6. *Finished drawing.* This is done in the office, usually for courtroom presentation in more serious crimes. Usually a trained draftsperson prepares this with drafting equipment and computer, using your field sketch as the reference for the more finished product. In cases where drawings of this type are prepared, it is not unusual for the prosecutor also to have scale models of the scene prepared for presentation.

Basic Rules for Sketching

Whether you estimate dimensions in your sketch or measure them, in all cases you must indicate which way you do it. It is not wise to mix measurements by estimating some and actually measuring others. Measurements must be precise when measured and the legend should state that they are exact. If you estimate measurements, be sure to put that in the legend as "all measurements are estimated." Even though you know for sure that your shoes are precisely eleven and a half inches long and you pace off twenty-three steps, you must state that all measurements are estimated and you would list the twenty-three paces as "approximately twenty-two feet."

Although a rough sketch will not be drawn to scale, it should be in proportion, so that there is less chance of distorted perception of the relative objects in the sketch. When you use a scale, try 1/2 inch = 1 foot for detailed sketches, or 1/4 inch = 1 foot for a larger scene. Try 1/8 inch = 1 foot for location sketches or 1/2 inch = 10 feet for larger areas. Whatever scale you use, try to keep the sketch on one sheet of paper to accompany your reports. Later you may choose to prepare a finished drawing on posterboard for courtroom presentation, but items that large are too cumbersome to place in file cabinets or to duplicate. You should also keep the sketch reasonably sized so that you may make transparencies for court presentation instead of using the larger boards.

1. *NORTH arrow.* In every sketch, you must include a NORTH arrow, or a symbol showing all four compass points, but the NORTH arrow is mandatory. It is best also to draw the sketch

so that NORTH is at the top of the page. One of your authors got lost in Paris once because the map provided by the hotel had west at the top instead of north and there was no compass anywhere on the map. As you know, just because the house is situated on North Alpine does not mean that the street goes north to south. Use a compass and indicate true north in your sketch. Although many photographers do not follow the procedure, may we suggest that you consider making a plywood or cardboard NORTH arrow to place in each scene you photograph.

2. *Title block or legend.* Either print it directly on your sketch or use a standardized card that you can attach securely to each sketch on which you print at least all of the following information: case number, date and time of the crime or collision, date and time the sketch is prepared, and by whom the sketch is prepared, including the person who took measurements (if measurements were taken). State the location of the event, including the street address (if any) and the exact place it took place (tennis court, living room, intersection, other). Indicate whether the sketch is to scale or estimated and what the scale is. Use a numbering and lettering system for evidence and photo spots, and list all those items in the legend space.

3. *Collision scene.* Show the exact point of impact, skid marks leading to that point, and the final resting place and position of the vehicle(s). Measure the width of the streets and sketch them in proportion to other objects in the sketch. Locate and identify the lights, signals, and traffic signs, such as "Speed Limit," or "Stop," or "Yield. " Name the streets and highways, locate and label vision obstructions that you observe, and list the type and condition of the road surface, such as "asphalt, wet from recent rain."

4. *Crime scene.* If the crime was committed in an open area, such as a public park or a front yard, show the locations where the parameter warning tapes or barricades were put up, familiar landmarks, and permanent objects at the location, such as trees and buildings. Be sure to sketch everything that appears to be related to the case.

   If the crime was committed inside a building, show the points of entry and exit, doors, windows, and large items of furniture and their relationship to each other and to the different

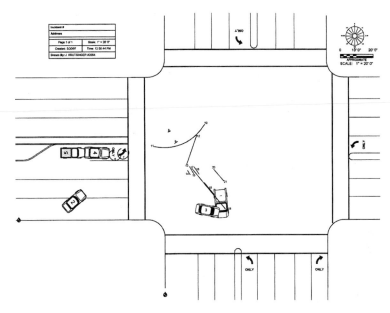

Figure 9.7   Traffic collision scene.

items of evidence. Sketches of crimes against persons should show the location where the assault took place, and a discarded weapon might be nearby. Sketches of crimes against property should show locations of pry marks and other trace evidence. Be sure to draw your sketch so that the information coincides with the information in your report and the numbers and letters assigned to the evidence and photos.

5. *Locating methods.* There are five methods for sketching the locations of various items of evidence used for crime and collision scene sketches. They are (a) straight line, (b) diagonal baseline, (c) coordinate, (d) polar coordinate, and (e) triangulation. The straight line method speaks for itself, measuring from one object to another and recording the distance. See Figure 9.8. For the diagonal baseline method, measure from an imaginary line that stretches diagonally from one corner of the room to the opposite corner and the distance from that line to the object, such as a tool or weapon.

For the coordinate method, draw a line and measure the distance from one wall to the item of evidence, and a line from the object to the wall at a right angle from the first wall, such as the east wall, then the south wall. For the polar coordinate

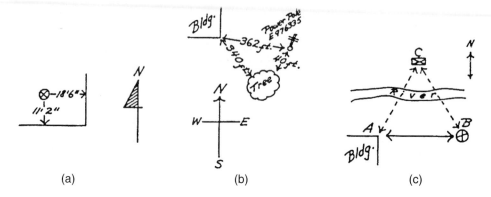

(a) (b) (c)

Figure 9.8 Measuring methods: (a) coordinates (b) polar coordinates (c) triangulation.

method, measure the distance from your object, such as a weapon, to a permanent fixture, such as a dishwasher (or a tree if outdoors), and another measurement from the evidence item to another large object that is not likely to be moved. For the triangulation method, draw a line from your evidence item to each of two permanent objects that are some distance apart. When you draw the lines from each stationary object to the third item you want to locate, it is possible to place the evidence in your sketch where the two lines from the permanent objects meet and cross each other.

SUMMARY

No matter how great a job you do searching for, and collecting evidence, nobody will know what kind of a job you have done unless you prepare accurate and complete reports, take good photographs, and draw sketches that explain themselves. The visual presentation is as important as the report, as they each complement the other, and they serve as memory joggers and scene management tools. There may be times when you will overlook a very crucial piece of evidence while conducting the initial search. Then later when you are reviewing the photographs (and videotape if you were able to use a camcorder), you will see what you missed, and you may be able to retrieve it before it is destroyed or disappears.

A professional athlete is only as good as his or her last game, coupled with the statistics. Your statistics will be based on how well you use these three tools in recording your investigation of crime scenes, the *report*, the *photographs*, and the *sketch*.

SUGGESTED OUTSIDE PROJECTS

1. Draw a sketch of an imaginary traffic collision scene involving two cars and a pickup truck with injuries involved. Draw a sketch of a burglary scene that appears to you to have been "rigged" by the "victim."

2. Take a thirty-six-exposure roll of photos of various items that might be considered evidence. Arrange the lighting, the flash, and focus the camera so that the pictures come out clear and distinct.

DISCUSSION QUESTIONS

1. What is the value of taking along a voice-actuated microcassette recorder while you are investigating a crime scene?

2. What is the advantage of videotaping the crime scene?

3. What is the purpose of putting in your report what you *do not* find during your investigation?

4. What is a "location shot"?

5. Why would you use a Polaroid camera if you have a perfectly good 35mm SLR camera?

6. Describe the sequence of photos you should take as you approach the crime scene.

7. What is the purpose of placing a ruler in close-up photos?

8. Do you think it is a good idea to put a NORTH arrow in a sketch?

9. Describe how you locate an object by triangulation.

10. Explain how you will present your photographs in court.

Chapter Ten
The Crime Lab

INTRODUCTION

After you complete your job at the crime scene and take the evidence you have collected to the laboratory, the criminalists and other technicians go to work. One word you will seldom if ever hear from those unsung heroes is *can't*. A forensics laboratory, or crime lab, as we usually call it, is more like a research lab rather a quality control lab, where minimum standards for certain products are maintained. What you will hear often is "let's give it a try." New discoveries are made almost every day in the crime labs around the world. For example, one of the most significant applications of DNA technology was done by an English doctor in a criminal case. In this chapter we will cover some of the basic instruments found in most crime labs and discuss some of the miracles criminalists can work with those instruments. For more detailed information on the science of criminalistics, check the references at the end of the book for some excellent books by the experts.

THE MICROSCOPE

Without a doubt, this is probably the most valuable instrument in the lab. It was certainly one of the first, which gave scientists the magnification necessary to examine substances that are impossible to study with the naked eye. The magnification can be almost without bounds. For example, the scanning electron microscope (SEM) magnifies an object over one hundred thousand times, whereas the standard lab microscope is considerably less, but still quite effective for many analyses. With the standard microscope it is possible to identify substances such as marijuana seeds and particles, weave characteristics of cloth, patterns of different species of wood and grains, rocks, minerals, sand, and soil.

With the aid of the microscope, criminalists can determine the presence of sperm and bacteria in semen and blood, and determine a person's blood type. They can identify materials, such as snagged clothing or traces of hair or blood, that adhere to a tool or weapon, or a bush or shrub. They also can tell you whether the substance is animal, vegetable, or mineral.

COMPARISON MICROSCOPE

The comparison microscope (or photomicrograph) is used to study the relative characteristics of bullets and the gun barrels they are believed to have been fired through. When the matching characteristics of the two are aligned, the expert will photograph the two magnified objects simultaneously so that the distinguishing characteristics that show the bullet probably traveled through that barrel. Handwriting exemplars can also be compared with the original writings, putting the images of the two side by side so that the expert can show their similarities to the investigators and eventually to the judge and/or jury at the trial.

BIOLOGICAL MICROSCOPE

The biological microscope magnifies material in two stages. The image is magnified first, then a second lens magnifies it further for a closer

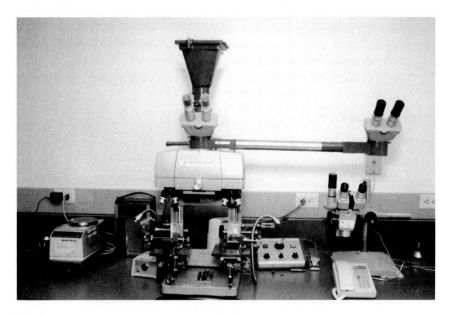

Figure 10.1 A comparison microscope with a 4 × 5 camera attached to the top.

examination. It is used by serologists for blood-typing and when searching for spermatozoa in blood in rape and sexual abuse cases. The expert also uses this instrument to examine the medulla, cortex, and scale patterns of hairs. Another common use of the biological microscope is to test for various drugs, narcotics, and other controlled substances.

STEREOSCOPIC BINOCULAR MICROSCOPE

The stereoscopic binocular microscope is used for almost any type of microscopic examination. This instrument has a separate microscope for each eye, giving the criminalist a three-dimensional view of the material under the glass.

BALLISTICS EXPERT

The ballistics expert uses a comparison microscope to compare bullets that are found in shooting crimes with bullets that he or she test-fires in the laboratory to look for similarities in their rifling and other marks made while they passed through the gun barrel. The ballistics expert will also

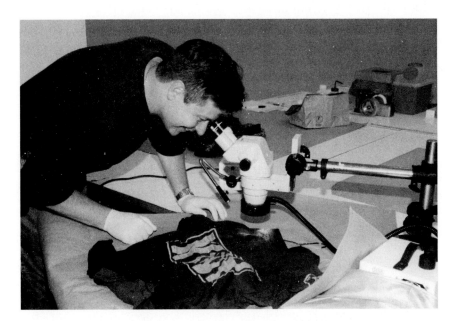

Figure 10.2   A stereoscopic microscope, which allows for three-dimensional viewing, is used here as small particles of lead are removed from around the hole in this homicide victim's clothing.

Figure 10.3a

Figure 10.3b   Large water tanks like these are used to collect firearm-related evidence. Often five or six feet of water is enough to stop a bullet while maintaining the striations needed for comparison.

use the same kind of gun that was fired at a crime scene, load it with the same type of ammunition, and fire into a piece of meat with the fatty side out to approximate a human being shot. The expert shoots from different angles to determine the angle of the shooter to the victim and different distances to determine how far the shooter was from the victim. When the fired bullet leaves the barrel of the gun, small shavings of the bullet and other residue from the blast also fly out of the barrel. The shavings will make a pattern of particles called *tattooing,* which will be embedded on the clothing and skin of the victim. The pattern is smaller the closer the gun is to the victim at the time it is fired. The microscope is used to facilitate this test as well.

The ballistics expert also examines the hands and clothing of the suspected shooter for residue from the explosion and can compare what he or she finds with similar materials on the victim and the gun.

GAS CHROMATOGRAPH

The gas chromatograph is used to identify the ingredients of liquid substances. The expert dilutes the liquid and injects it into the intake port of the instrument. With few exceptions, most compounds are different although they may contain the same ingredients. For example, there is enough difference between Texaco gasoline and Shell gasoline that samples of those brands can be compared with the suspected substance and identified as one or the other gasoline product. An exception to this would be the independent gas station that buys surplus gasoline from whichever company it can get the best price, and its gas tanks may have a mixture of three or four different brands of gasoline.

The gas chromatograph scans over four hundred different ions and weighs them, then prints out a graph with several different patterns of lines, each pattern representing a different compound. The contents of a kerosene can found at the home of a suspect may be compared with the flammable material used to start an arson fire that you found on the charred wood at the point where the fire was started. The two charts will compare positively, giving the criminalist a probable match.

SPECTROPHOTOMETER

A spectrographic analysis will be used to examine traces or fragments of materials found at the crime scene, and the analysis is recorded on photographic film. The substance in question is burned, which disturbs its characteristic atomic structure. Each substance burns with different colors unique to that substance. The colors are actually waves of energy expressed in color. This light is projected through a prism onto the photographic plate. If black-and-white film is used, the light variations will be printed onto the photographic film as a series of parallel lines of varying density from light gray to black. When color film is used the bands will show up as different colors of the spectrum. Each substance will cast a different arrangement of the lines, and the expert will be able to identify the materials being examined.

NEUTRON ACTIVATION ANALYSIS

The specimen is bombarded with a stream of neutrons and the instrument measures the wavelength and intensity of the radiation given off by the substances that have been made radioactive by the neutrons. At least seventy different elements can be identified and quantitatively determined by measurement of the interaction of their stable isotopes with the neutrons, known as radionuclides, as they decay. This result appears as lines on the chart that resemble peaks and valleys, which the criminalist studies and interprets various patterns as specific elements.

Figure 10.4   The laboratory can utilize many processing techniques that cannot be done in the field.

WET CHEMISTRY

When you are discussing all of the instrumentation in the laboratory, do not overlook the value of chemistry to forensic science. Many suspected substances can be isolated and identified by mixing them with specific chemical formulae, or *reagents*. With wet chemistry it is possible to identify thousands of substances, including drugs, narcotics, and blood. Through chemistry, the expert can determine whether the blood is animal or human, and which animal. Blood types and DNA are determined with the aid of blood analysis. You may have been provided a collection of *reagents* in different vials so that you can conduct field tests for drugs, blood, and other liquids. When the suspected liquid is dropped into the reagent, the reagent changes colors, and you can tell what the suspected liquid is by what color and shade it changes into.

X-RAY

The X-ray is a better and safer way to look into a package without opening it, especially when the package contains a bomb or other dangerous material. Used extensively for airport security for several years, the X-ray can speed up the passenger screening process by looking into most containers without opening them. The container should be nonmetallic, and the metal objects inside will show up in silhouette on the screen.

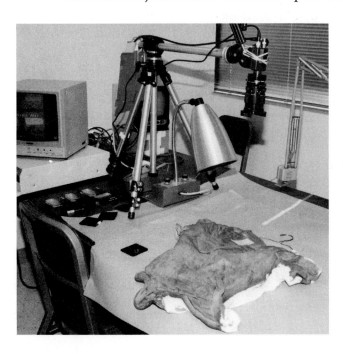

Figure 10.5   Infrared video is used to document gunshot residue on clothing that is invisible to the naked eye.

Valuable original paintings that have been painted over with another painting will show up in X-ray, as the newer painting will be more transparent than the older one. Jewelers and appraisers as well as jewel theft officers use X-ray to examine diamonds, pearls, and other gemstones to verify their authenticity and their value in addition to the usual method of using the ten power loop for examination and appraisal.

X-ray diffraction photography (the photo is called a radiograph and in the medical lab the expert is known as a radiologist) will distinguish objects that are chemically identical but differ in atomic arrangement. Auto grease stains, for example, can be distinguished from other grease compounds, such as kitchen grease. Barbiturates can be identified and compared with X-ray diffraction.

INFRARED

Infrared light can be used to make some things appear that would otherwise be invisible or nearly invisible. Infrared heat sensors are used by the military and the police as to look into the darkness to search for living objects, particularly humans who are missing or lost, or who might be trying to evade detection in the dark. Obliterated writings on surfaces that have been inked over may be made visible because the original writing shines through the overwriting under the infrared light. With the use of infrared light you may be able to read the letter inside an envelope without having to steam the envelope open or breaking the seal. If an erasure

Figure 10.6   Here a laser beam is used to show bullet trajectory in this example. The laser is useful in that its range is nearly endless and, more importantly, perfectly straight.

is not complete, you may find that you can bring out the erased writing with infrared.

A very popular type of pointer is the one that beams an infrared beam across the room. This is the same type of pointer that can be attached to a handgun, a rifle, or a shotgun and lighted to point to the spot where the bullets will strike the target. Infrared is also used for night vision cameras and binoculars.

ULTRAVIOLET

Some substances, such as semen, rouge, and lipstick, will fluoresce under ultraviolet light. Urine, milk, saliva, and erased writings will become visible under ultraviolet light. If you have a multicolored surface and cannot bring up latent prints because of the conflicting colors, use fluorescent fingerprint powder instead of the customary powder and the prints will glow quite distinctly under the ultraviolet light. Many different inks and papers will fluoresce under the light, and undercover officers will make buys of contraband with money marked with inks and dies that are invisible to the naked eye, which fluoresce under ultraviolet. Many aerosol tear gas and pepper spray manufacturers mix in a dye that also fluoresces under the light.

EVIDENCE VACUUM

In the crime lab you will find one or more vacuum cleaners that have been sterilized and equipped with a special clean filter. The technicians vacuum clothing of suspected narcotics users and dealers for residue or powder from the pockets and surface, and they vacuum other places for narcotics or controlled substances. The sterile filter will insure that matter collected by the vacuum comes only from the place the technician vacuums.

SOUND SPECTROGRAPH

This device is more commonly known as the *voice print analyzer*. Voice patterns are transformed into visual patterns on a graph that moves through the instrument at a controlled speed, and patterns are drawn on the paper as it moves. By comparing the print patterns of two people who sound alike to you and me, the expert can tell you which one is the impersonator of the other. By analyzing the charts, some manufacturers claim, you can compare a tape of an individual's "normal" speech pattern with a tape of the same person being questioned about his or her involvement in some type of crime or other misbehavior. You can tell that the person is stressed and probably untruthful. Such a device has yet to be used in a courtroom, where many people are known to have lied under oath.

AUTOMATED FINGERPRINT SYSTEMS (AFS)

Since fingerprints were first used for identification purposes and classification systems were developed for indexing and searching the files for comparison purposes, fingerprint technology has been the most consistently reliable method for positively identifying the owner of a set of prints. To this date, no two people have been found to have identical fingerprints. When you send latents to the laboratory and also submit all the elimination prints that you took of victims and witnesses at the scene, the technicians will try for a match (or elimination) with all the prints you submitted. Then the technician takes advantage of the automated fingerprint systems that connect your department with virtually every other department that is connected to the system. If there is a match, it will take only a few minutes compared with the months or years it would take an expert to search the files. We have already covered fingerprints in Chapter Eight.

DNA ANALYSIS

The genetic fingerprint of an individual is so unique that the experts are projecting that it is impossible for any two people, except identical twins, to have identical genetic codes. Blood, hair follicles, bones, tissue, body

Figure 10.7   This Automated Fingerprint Identification System, or AFS, workstation can search unknown fingerprints against a database of millions of known suspects.

fluids, and almost any cell of a person's body will yield sufficient data so that the laboratory can yield sufficient data so that the laboratory can identify the owner and match it to materials found at the scene. This discovery has made it possible for people in prison to be freed many years after their conviction because DNA tests show that they were not the ones who committed the crimes, and other suspects have been located and their DNA matched. Some larger departments have teams of officers assigned to long-time unsolved murders, some cases still open for over twenty years, and they are solving some of those crimes with the aid of DNA analysis. DNA is also used to identify remains of people whose bodies have decayed so far that bone marrow samples are used to determine their DNA and their identity. In 1997 Nicholas II, czar of Russia, and his family, killed by communist revolutionaries in 1918, were finally identified by their DNA and given a royal funeral in July 1998. Their DNA was determined by taking samples of their bone marrow and comparing it to that of Prince Philip, husband of Queen Elizabeth of England and a direct descendant of the czar.

The application of DNA science to crime investigation has been one of the great discoveries of the twentieth century, and it promises to be a tremendous ally during the twenty-first century. Eyewitnesses make mistakes, but fingerprints and DNA do not.

FORENSIC TOXICOLOGY

The toxicologist studies the fluids and organs of the bodies of living or deceased persons and attempts to identify toxic substances that cause illness or death. This expert has an extensive knowledge of drugs and poisons and is called upon frequently to apply his or her skills to criminal homicide and other drug-related crimes.

FORENSIC ANTHROPOLOGY

This scientist is called upon to examine bodies and body parts in various states of decomposition or in their whole condition. Through a study of the bones and whatever remains of the body, the anthropologist determines whether it is animal or human. These scientists have been known to estimate the approximate age, sex, race, height, weight, period of time since the person died, and nature of skeletal injuries sustained by the victim. Sometimes the anthropologist can reconstruct a face over the skull that will give investigators a fair idea what the victim looked like before death. The anthropologist can tell if bones belong to the same person and can take samples of bone marrow to send to a DNA laboratory for possible identification of the deceased.

COMPOSITE DRAWINGS, COMPUTER IMAGING

Eyewitnesses are often asked to work with a sketch artist or an expert who attempts to recreate an image of the suspect. Every department does not have access to an artist, but many departments have a composite specialist who may use a computer or a collection of transparencies. From the description provided by the witness, the specialist selects face shape and size, then adds a hairline and hairstyle, eyes and ears, and so forth until the piece-by-piece construction of the suspect's face resembles the description provided by the witness. One of the earlier composite kits in the 1950s consisted of a box full of line drawings on transparent sheets of plastic. There were transparencies of eyes, noses, ears, chins, heads, hair, and other parts of the face that were used to put the composite together. Many improvements have been made since then, including utilization of the computer to prepare the image. A real treasure is to have an artist who can take the composite, then add scars or tattoos, and fill in the composite to make a finished product that resembles a more realistic likeness of the suspect.

Figure 10.8   A PC-based digital imaging workstation.

POLYGRAPH, THE LIE DETECTOR

This "many graph" instrument measures and records body functions, which are drawn onto a chart that moves through the instrument at a measured rate. The lie detector is the person who operates the instrument, and the examiner's competency determines the reliability of the polygraph. Although the polygraph has been around for many years (one of your authors was qualified as an examiner in 1960), it is not admissible in court except by stipulation of the judge and both attorneys, and its principal function is as an investigative tool.

The polygraph measures and records pulse, blood pressure, respiration, certain body movements, and galvanic skin response, or the changes in a small electric current sent through the body by way of electrodes attached to one finger in each hand. As the examiner asks questions that must be answered with only a "yes" or "no," the pens are recording on the chart the various body functions. As each question is asked and answered with an affirmative or negative response, the examiner makes note of changes in pulse, respiration, blood pressure, the GSR (galvanic skin response), and squirming or similar body movements (all instruments do not have sensors under the subject's legs to record body movements). After a series of questions that the subject knows of in advance, the examiner will repeat the test once or twice and then analyze the chart. If certain changes on the chart appear to coincide with the answers given, the examiner may interpret the physical changes as emotional reactions to the question and answer. The interpreter then determines whether these changes indicate deception or not. The principle of the polygraph is based on the belief that most people have a conscience and that they cannot lie to themselves. When they do lie, they have inner turmoil, which shows on the charts as changes in the body functions. The tests are conducted in a clinical atmosphere, and the only two people in the room during the test are the examiner and the subject.

PRINT AND TRACE EXPERTS

In the larger forensics laboratories, there are experts who specialize in such subjects as footwear identification and comparison, tire impressions, blood spatters, and mechanical matching of broken pieces of evidence. Most departments do not have the luxury of such a breakdown in specialties, and it is not uncommon for each criminalist in the lab to be a triple threat, doubling up on his or her competencies as an expert. A hair and fiber analyst may also work with soils and rocks, for example, whereas all are usually experts with wet chemistry and the use of the microscope.

SUMMARY

The crime laboratory is very much like an experimental lab. Even though they may be carrying a heavy load already, most of the experts in the lab do the best they can to help the investigators solve the crime. Before you are assigned to investigate crime scenes as a specialty, you should visit several of the crime labs in your area and see how the criminalists work so that you may hone your CSI skills and you will have a better understanding what the lab can and cannot do.

SUGGESTED OUTSIDE PROJECTS

1. Visit the largest forensics lab in your area and take along with you the list of instruments and services described in this chapter. Compare our list with what you find on your visit. What does the lab have that we did not mention? How do they use the instruments? Write to the authors of this book with your findings so that we may update our next edition.

2. Take a polygraph exam. Some local examiner probably will be glad to use you as a subject to demonstrate how it works. Write a paper on how the polygraph works and whether you believe the results of a test should be admissible in court or not.

DISCUSSION QUESTIONS

1. List five types of evidence that are examined in the lab with the standard microscope.

2. Explain how two bullets are compared in a ballistics test.

3. For what kind of a case would the lab use the gas chromatograph?

4. What instrument would you use to find out if a valuable painting by one of the masters, such as van Gogh, had been painted over to smuggle it out of the country?

5. What are some uses of infrared light?

6. For what types of cases would the lab use ultraviolet light?

7. What is the probability of two people having the same DNA, or genetic code?

8. According to the text, how accurate is the polygraph? What does your instructor say about the accuracy of the polygraph?

9. Can an anthropologist determine the sex of the deceased by examining his or her skeleton?

10. What is a comparison microscope, and how does it work?

Chapter Eleven
Going To Court

INTRODUCTION

Your job is not done until you have performed another very important function in the crime scene investigation. That function is testifying in court and presenting the evidence that you discovered and processed. You are the first link in the chain of custody, and your role is to make your presentation and testimony factually and without embellishment. As you know, the criminal trial is an adversarial proceeding where prosecution and defense attorneys fight a pitched battle to get the results that they are paid to by representing their clients to the best of their ability. Your role in this battle is not the same as that of the attorneys. Your role is to present your evidence and testimony professionally and impartially so that the judge and jury will have your contribution to the case to determine truth, legality, and guilt or innocence. Too many officers who testify in court assume an adversarial stance the minute they get on the stand, purring like well-oiled machinery and presenting their testimony in a friendly and businesslike manner while being questioned by the prosecutor. Then, when the defense attorney gets up to cross-examine the officer, you can actually see the change in that officer's attitude. The officer will assume a defensive position physically, such as holding the hands together or folding the arms, and actually change facial expressions as though the defense attorney were the devil himself. Hostility and reluctant cooperation replace friendly and businesslike manner, which is readily apparent to all who observe the transition.

Actually, in some cases you might receive a subpoena from the defense attorney to be a witness for the "other side," as you see it. Keep in mind that your role is not to take sides with either prosecution or defense. You represent truth and fact, and your presentation should be a forthright and businesslike presentation of the facts with *truth* being your own ally. You may sometimes be required to give testimony that is favorable to the defense (heaven forbid, you think), but remember the rule of evidence that "evidence suppressed is presumed to be favorable to the defense." It is not your responsibility to find the defendant guilty or to administer the punishment. Your job simply is to tell the truth.

THE SUBPOENA

When you receive a subpoena, check out all the information about the case to see if it is one that you had anything to do with. Sometimes the attorneys do not prepare the subpoenas; they leave it up to a clerk in the office, who issues subpoenas for every person named in the report if they are not familiar with the case. You may have been driving by a crime scene being investigated by a colleague and advised that your assistance was not needed, but your name was put in the report because you offered your services and then left the scene. Another example would be such a statement as: "We questioned the suspect in Sergeant Quimby's office," and you are Quimby. You were not even in the office that day and the officers used your office because you were on vacation. But you still get a subpoena. Notify the office of the attorney that issued the subpoena and have the office excuse you. Do not ignore the subpoena, as you could be arrested for contempt for not showing up in court.

If the case is one that you investigated, review all of your notes, the reports, and check to see what has been done with all the evidence. Although some attorneys are too busy to talk with you until the actual day of the trial, we suggest that you contact the attorney who subpoenaed you, tell him or her that you are prepared, and set up a time for a pretrial consultation.

PRETRIAL CONFERENCE

Meet with the attorney and discuss all of the evidence and testimony that you are going to bring to the trial. When you talk over the case, don't leave anything out. There should be no last-minute surprises when you are on the stand, such as revealing information that you did not give to the attorney. One good rule for attorneys is that they should never ask a question without knowing the answer. This conference is primarily for the attorney to find out what kind of a witness you are going to be and to plan strategy so that you will be called upon for your contribution at a logistically and strategically good time during the trial.

EXPERT OR EXPERIENCED?

Because of your education, training, and experience in police investigative matters, you know more about what you do than the average person on the street, or the average police officer for that matter, and you would probably be considered an expert. As an expert you are qualified by the court to go beyond presentation of your perceptions, to also render opinions in categories of your expertise. This extra privilege to be qualified as an expert may sound good, and indeed may be good for your presentation. Yet this is a two-sided "monster" in some cases. For example, as an expert crime scene investigator, you may be asked by a defense attorney about the qualifications and performance of other officers at the scene. If one of those officers really "screwed up" and you know that he or she did a rotten job, as a lay witness you present your testimony and evidence and leave. You will not be asked about your opinions of the competency of your colleagues. But, as an expert, you may have to point out how your colleague messed up the investigation so badly that you were afraid that the whole case would be lost. Whether the prosecutor will have you take *voir dire* and have the court recognize you as an expert is up to the prosecutor. Discuss that matter before you get on the stand and are sworn in.

If you are presented as an expert, be sure to do your homework and be prepared to answer all kinds of questions about your area of expertise, whether related to the current case or not. Good attorneys would not be worth their salt if they did not try to discredit you on the stand. Your authors have testified as lay police witnesses and as experts, and they have found that each case is different and that the attorneys should plan the strategy of how they are going to use you as a witness.

WAITING TO TESTIFY

When you arrive in court, be sure to let the attorney who called you know that you are present and available. If the attorney is not going to get to you for a while, you may ask to be put *on call*, so that you can go back home or to your job and wait to be called with about a half hour's notice, or more, depending on how far you will be from the courthouse. The attorney may or may not consult with you at that time about your testimony and the evidence you are going to present. You may be required by the court to wait outside the courtroom while others testify. This is usually a move made by a defense attorney who does not want two partners in a case to hear each other's testimony so that they can synchronize their testimony. You are outside while your partner is testifying, then you are called to the stand while he or she is meeting you in the aisle on the way out, giving you no time to compare notes. Don't worry about your testimony not being exactly the same. If you are telling the truth from your own perspective, there is no doubt that there are going to be inconsistencies because you each interpret your observations through your own cognitive system.

While waiting outside the courtroom for your turn to testify, it is better not to strike up conversations with other people who are waiting outside for similar purposes. You never know who you are talking to, and it could prove embarrassing if you were to reveal information that the other person should not know. The best advice is to keep your own counsel while waiting to testify.

TESTIFYING AS A WITNESS

Now is your time to shine! Everyone has stage fright before and during his or her appearance as a witness. You may be shaking and sweating, and for that you should be thankful. It shows that the adrenal glands are working, and the adrenaline pumping through your body will prepare you for this unusual event. Public speakers, teachers, athletes, and performers all experience this "rush," and most learn to use it to their advantage, as it sharpens your senses and increases your capabilities.

Whether you should wear a uniform in court depends on what you usually wear while on duty in your regular assignment. If you work in street clothes, then you will not be required to go out and buy a new uniform because the old one does not fit anymore. If you wear a uniform on duty, wear a clean and neatly pressed one to testify. The judge may have specific requirements about sidearms and may require that you hand any weapon you might be wearing to the bailiff when you enter, and the bailiff will return it to you when you depart.

If you are required to wait in the spectator area behind the bar, be careful not to draw attention to yourself by waving to other officers or making obscene gestures to the defendant. Until you are called before the bar to the witness stand to testify, your demeanor should be that of a disinterested bystander. You have no personal axe to grind, and you are there as a witness, not an adversary.

When you are called to the witness stand, you will be required to take the oath or affirm that your testimony will be truthful. Please take that oath seriously and speak only the truth during your testimony. In the authors' opinion, for an officer to lie from the witness stand in court is as bad as a minister blaspheming God from the pulpit. Answer all questions as they are put to you. If you do not hear or do not understand a question, say so. Give your answer then keep quiet. The attorneys will ask for an expansion of your reply or ask you to explain an answer if they choose to. It is their show. Sometimes an overzealous witness will start offering answers to questions that have not yet been asked, or which will never be asked because the attorneys have reasons for running the examination as they are. There is a time and place for certain information to be given or evidence to be presented, and that should be left up to the attorneys.

EXAMINATION AND CROSS-EXAMINATION

During the direct examination by the attorney who called you as a witness, usually the prosecutor, the attorney will ask you questions that can be answered with a "yes," a "no," or a narrative response, such as "Now that you testified that you were at that location on the night of August 14 at 9 P.M., tell the jury what you saw." The attorney is not allowed to ask leading or argumentative questions during direct examination in most cases. An exception to this is if the witness is noncooperative and the attorney will then ask the judge to approve questioning of the witness as a "hostile witness." The general rule for testifying is to answer the questions and present your evidence as the attorney asks you to do, and don't volunteer any additional information.

After the prosecutor is finished questioning you, the defense attorney will cross-examine you. The purpose of cross-examination is to challenge the truthfulness and accuracy of a witness. Be prepared to answer leading questions such as: "Officer Virtue, isn't it true that you actually arrived at the scene at 9:30, and not 8:30 as you testified during direct examination?" The general rule for answering questions during cross-examination is the same as for direct examination: Answer fully and honestly without trying to explain an answer unless asked to do so, and do not volunteer answers to questions that are not asked. The defense attorney may try to make you angry or confused, and perhaps say things without thinking. Be careful, because some attorneys love to badger police witnesses, and, I suspect, some judges who love to see the badgering going on. A judge is less likely to interfere when an attorney is giving a police officer witness a bad time than if the witness were a child or a woman or another lay witness.

USE OF NOTES

Consult with the attorney before you refer to any notes that you have brought with you. Show the attorney what you are going to use to refresh your memory when necessary, but don't "spring" notes on him or her from your pocket without any advance notice. Also, before you testify from those notes or any other document, the opposing attorney must have the opportunity to examine them. Use your notes and reports whenever you need them to assure accuracy in your testimony. If your notes regarding that particular case are in a book that includes notes about other cases or other information concerning your work or private life, those portions may be blocked off by paper clips or staples. Contrary to popular belief, attorneys have no right and no business to go through the parts of your notebook that are not directly related to the case in hand or that you are using to refresh your memory.

TESTIMONY IN OTHER MATTERS

You may be called upon to testify during preliminary hearings, pretrial motion hearings, coroners' inquests, or administrative hearings, such as for workers' compensation or a school board. The rules are generally the same as far as responding to a subpoena and testifying during the proceedings. The prosecutor will point out to you the minor differences, such as hearsay is not admissible in a trial, but an experienced officer may testify to hearsay during certain preliminary proceedings. Some proceedings are more formal than others, but your demeanor should always be that of the professional police witness whose sole duty it is to present the facts in a concise and factual manner.

SUMMARY

You will be required to present your evidence and testimony in court as the final step in your crime scene investigation process. The general rule to follow is to be on time, be professional, and be truthful. Always remember that you are a witness and not an adversary. Your testimony and evidence should speak for themselves as to your honesty and efficiency, and any impassioned plea to the emotions of one side or the other will not enhance your image as a professional crime scene investigator. Be prompt, be honest, and be seated. Then, when you have finished testifying, ask the judge if you may be excused and leave. Don't hang around after you have testified to make sure the "scumbag gets his due." Read about it in the newspaper the next day or call the prosecutor in a day or two and ask about the outcome of the case. Not only must you be impersonal and professional in your persona, but you must be those things in the eyes of others.

SUGGESTED OUTSIDE PROJECTS

1. Spend at least fifteen hours at a trial or visit three short trials for a total of fifteen hours. Pay particular attention to the professionals who testify, such as police officers and expert witnesses. Write a critique on their performances and their behavior in the courtroom before and after testifying.

2. In this chapter we did not cover appearance before the grand jury. Visit your local prosecutor and ask how a witness would be handled for an appearance before that tribunal. What about examination and cross-examination, or is there any cross-examination if attorneys are not allowed to be present during witness testimony?

DISCUSSION QUESTIONS

1. When you receive a subpoena, describe what you must do before you go to court.

2. How does a witness qualify as an expert witness?

3. How does the testimony of an expert witness differ from that of a lay witness?

4. Why are witnesses sometimes required to wait outside the courtroom until it is time for them to testify?

5. Why ask the judge to excuse you after you testify as a witness?

6. How would you go about getting to use your notes during your testimony?

7. What do the authors mean when they say that a trial is an *adversary hearing*?

8. If you receive a subpoena and find that you had nothing to do with the case, what do you do?

9. What types of questions may be asked during a direct examination?

10. What types of questions can be asked during cross-examination?

For Further Study

Bodziak, William J. *Footwear Impression Evidence.* Boca Raton, Florida: CRC Press Inc., 1995.

CA Criminalist Institute. "Latent Print Comparisons." Classroom text/handouts, n.d. California Department of Justice, Sacramento.

CA Criminalist Institute. "Latent Print Techniques." Classroom text/handouts, n.d. California Department of Justice, Sacramento.

Cassidy, Michael. *Footwear Identification.* Ottawa, Canada: RCMP GRC, 1987.

Hilderbrand, Dwane S. "Footwear, The Missed Evidence." Classroom text/handouts, n.d. California Department of Justice, Sacramento.

Redsicker, David R. *The Practical Methodology of Forensic Photography.* New York, New York: Elsevier Science Publishing, 1991.

Smith, Ron. "Demystifying Palm Prints." Classroom text/handouts, n.d. California Department of Justice, Sacramento.

Staff, FBI Carl Collins. "FSI Advanced Latent Fingerprint School." Classroom text/handouts, n.d. FBI, Washington, DC.

Index